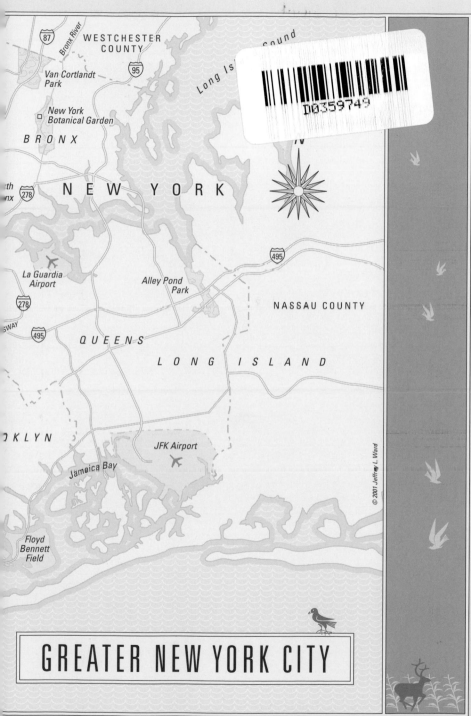

GREATER NEW YORK CITY

Y03

ID359749

© 2001 Jeffrey L. Ward

Also by Anne Matthews

Where the Buffalo Roam

Bright College Years

Wild Nights

Wild Nights

Nature Returns to the City

Anne Matthews

North Point Press

A division of Farrar, Straus and Giroux

New York

North Point Press
A division of Farrar, Straus and Giroux
19 Union Square West, New York 10003

Copyright © 2001 by Anne Matthews
All rights reserved
Distributed in Canada by Douglas & McIntyre Ltd.
Printed in the United States of America
First edition, 2001

Library of Congress Cataloging-in-Publication Data
Matthews, Anne, 1957–
    Wild nights : nature returns to the city / Anne Matthews.— 1st ed.
        p.   cm.
    ISBN 0-86547-560-1 (hc. : alk. paper)
    1. Urban ecology (Biology)—New York (State)—New York.
    2. Urban animals—New York (State)—New York.   I. Title.

QH105.N7 M38 2001
577.5'6'097471—dc21

                                                                00-049626

Designed by Jonathan D. Lippincott

The city! The city! To live elsewhere is mere eclipse.
—Cicero

You may drive nature out with a pitchfork,
but she will always hasten back.
—Horace

Rowing in Eden—
Ah! the sea! . . .
Wild nights should be
Our luxury.
—Emily Dickinson

Contents

Wild Nights

Introduction

In the first week of my first year in Greater New York, I hid a twenty-dollar bill in my shoe and took New Jersey Transit to The City, as everyone in Princeton seemed to call it; you could hear the capital letters every time. Another new graduate student from Wisconsin came with me, grumbling. If you are young and ambitious and live west of the Mississippi, Los Angeles and Seattle pull at the imagination far more strongly than the old cities of the eastern seaboard. But Madison lies just within New York's thousand-mile forcefield. So this was really a courtesy visit, we assured each other as the train rattled cityward through Linden and Rahway, because back home we were already terrific urbanites, who gloried in each fat Sunday *New York Times*; had seen (though never eaten) a water bagel; had visited Chicago on bus trips since junior high.

But New York undid us. Three blocks from Penn Station, at Broadway and Herald Square, we clung together in a Macy's doorway, stunned, disoriented, drowning. Even when we shouted we could not hear each other; almost nothing is louder than midtown Manhattan, not even a jet engine at close range. The gray urban air smelled of sewers and diesel and burned pushcart chestnuts. The local signage was full of opinions: LITTERING IS FILTHY AND SELFISH. DON'T EVEN *THINK* ABOUT PARKING HERE. And no matter which way I looked to find a horizon, I saw only faces—near, nearer, gone: Manhattan wedges 1.5 million residents plus three million commuters onto a granite island thirteen miles long by two miles wide. A band of city pigeons made a showy landing at the curb, barged over, and began to eat our shoelaces.

At least, they looked like pigeons; in truth, these were feral superdoves—immigrant New Yorkers descended from Old World rock doves and escaped racing birds, honed to urban perfection by urban pressures. New York City pigeons can breed year-round, eat meat, and see ultraviolet light. They perform alarmingly well on tests of symbolic logic. They produce droppings acid enough to snap the cables of the Brooklyn Bridge. I looked down at the iridescent necks of the flock surging about my ankles and up at the impossible Manhattan skyline and began to understand that in this magnificent and unforgiving place, this American Galapagos, adaptation—change—is the only law and only hope. My compatriot went home at midyear. He said the New York region was clearly uncivilized; you couldn't even get the noon farm prices on the radio. I stayed, became a commuter, and learned to barge and peck.

But after twenty years spent in and around America's largest city, I began to notice odd alterations in the texture of daily life here, little slubs in the weave. No hog futures on the radio yet, but definitely a spate of wildlife reports—animal, vegetable, and mineral. A cornfield appeared on Upper Broadway. A Dominican immigrant had noticed a nice piece of land going to waste, there in the median strip, and decided to farm it; the city let him. When a distinctly under-the-weather fox visited the inner suburbs, its cityward progress was breathlessly chronicled on New York's all-news stations (". . . to see what a fox looks like, especially a rabid one, go straight to our Web site at www.1010.WINS!"). By 1999, coyotes and wild turkeys had begun to roam Central Park. ("How did they get there?" demanded *The Wall Street Journal.* "Crosstown bus?") By 2000, black bear had visited suburban Chappaqua, and the Palisades Parkway. White-tailed deer came back to Manhattan for the first time in generations, making late-night dashes down the Amtrak trestle at the tidal strait called Spuyten Duyvil, on the island's north end, where Henry Hudson once came ashore.

And between Newark and the Jersey Meadowlands one winter morning, I spotted from my train window a dozen egrets, flying low above the dank chemical mudflats, an arrow of white headed straight for the World Trade Center. What are they *doing* here? I wondered, horrified, amazed. How do they *live*? But a quarter-century of water cleanup has brought ibis and yellow-crowned night herons and the shy and solitary bittern back to that former open sewer, New York Harbor. Hundreds of herons now breed on uninhabited islands off the Bronx and Queens and Staten Island. To see them, you must crawl ashore through great tangles of poison ivy, then hold up a truck mirror to observe their secret rookeries—but they're there, and flourishing. I had no idea.

It was a figure-ground problem, really. For years, I had looked at Greater New York and seen only what I expected: a profoundly unnatural landscape; a competitive maze; a wonder of money and art that seemed a thrilling human triumph on some days, and on others, a declensionist's delight. New York attracts jeremiads. Emerson called it a sucked orange; Fitzgerald pronounced its grimy suburban sprawl "the ugliest country in the world"; Vonnegut thought it a skyscraper national park. Yet above, around, behind, below, I began to find another New York, suppressed or silent in daylight, exceedingly lively from twilight to dawn.

Because I am interested in how place shapes people, and vice versa, over the last eight years I have been writing books— as a reporter, as a participant-observer, as a witness—about American landscapes in the grip of change, like the Great Plains, like the college campus: for both, deciding who and what must alter stirred the deepest passions and the worst fights. Yet all the while I was living in Greater New York, of all American landscapes the most transformed and conflicted, the best studied, and the least understood. Four years ago, when I started gathering material for *Wild Nights*, much of it seemed academic speculation, or outright fantasy, like the damage projections for a Manhattan-bound hurricane, or researchers' solemn warnings on the migratory potential of jet-age viruses. Yet as fictions turn to fact, and theories become headlines, the range of potential futures for The City—any city—becomes daily more distinct. Some urban futures are reassuring, others dire. But nearly all evoke our species' ancient dread of nature coming back to a human-claimed place: the return, the retaking. The book's first section ("Sky and Water") considers the mystery of nature's resurgence in the urban and suburban landscapes of the twenty-first century. Part II ("Leaf and Stone") traces the history of the nature/culture shoving match that so distinctively shaped greater New York. The final section ("Day and Night") suggests some outcomes for this new and baffling wilderness: the contingencies, the competing visions, the odds for us all.

For human and nonhuman to covet the same real estate is no light matter, since the next decades will be the first truly urban period in human history. At the turn of the twenty-first century, half of us were concentrated in the world's metropolitan areas, particularly twenty or so emerging supercities, chief among them New York, Los Angeles, London, Rio, Mexico City, Djakarta, Calcutta, Lagos, Nairobi, and Dacca. By 2050, three-fourths of our species will be city creatures. Already, about one American in fifteen lives in New York, or in the New York suburbs.

Yet throughout the United States, as from Toronto to Tokyo, nature/culture confrontation is becoming part of urban, suburban, and periurban routine. Some encounters in this new wilderness charm us; some we dread; others we badly misunderstand. Archaeology, history, and the earth sciences all tell us that other citified cultures, in other centuries, met such tests too. Most failed—some gradually, some with spectacular rapidity—for reasons already repeating themselves in the five boroughs today, and in the fifty states. Messing too much with the natural world generally hands an urban culture one of three outcomes: a transformed life, a lesser life, a long night.

New York has long cultivated an edgy relationship with nature, that big green blur between the lobby and the cab. To be vague or dismissive about the resurgent natural world is the last acceptable prejudice in The City, which talks a lot about diversity, but about biodiversity hardly at all. Yet the array of new pressures already hard upon New York are all environmental, from regional hyperdevelopment to the effects of climate change on an island metropolis. New York, that fashion-forward town, has never minded change, if it can set the terms—a luxury that may no longer be possible. For centuries now, the city of New York has resolutely rushed ahead, determined to find the best deal, to never waste time, to never show weakness. It rarely looks around, rarely looks back. Maybe it should. Wild does not always mean natural; urban is not the same as tame. Even in Manhattan, you are never more than three feet from a spider.

One

Sky and Water

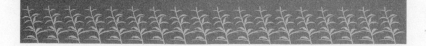

Wall Street Losses

By two in the morning, New York is as quiet as it gets. You can walk for blocks up Broadway and hardly see a moving car; you can stand at the corner of Forty-second and Fifth and, sometimes, smell the sea. By three in the morning, the planet's most profoundly developed real estate has nearly shimmered back into its earliest self, forty rocky islands set in river, bay, and sound. Rikers, Swinburne, Black Bank, Plum. North Brother, and Castle, and Cuban Ledge. The Isle of Meadow. Ellis, and Coney. Long Island, where Brooklyn elbows Queens. Staten. Manhattan.

Of New York's five great boroughs, only the Bronx is part of the North American continent, and it contains both the worst slums and the best stand of virgin timber in New York City. Manhattan is the most densely populated New York borough, Staten Island the most rural, Brooklyn the most populous. Queens is the largest in area and the most ethnically varied, even in a city where 40 percent of the residents are foreign-born.

Sky and Water

By four in the morning, each member of this urban archipelago sails alone. To go directly from Wall Street to Staten Island now, you almost need a kayak, or a canoe; the New York airports are all silent, the commuter ferries rock at pierside, and the river tunnels have nearly emptied too, their fluorescent lights fizzing peach and ice-white and spring-green fifty feet below the Hudson, churned by twice-a-day tides from sweet to salt. A few tropical butterfly fish, gold and silver, black and white, are dozing beneath the city's piers and pilings, their colors dimmed as they rest. Warm Atlantic currents sweep coral-reef species into the New York estuary every year. Sea turtles (some the size of hubcaps, others half the size of full-grown steers) can be in the harbor too, dragged in by tankers or lost on migration. These do not care for city life, so the local coast guard has become proficient at turtle rescue and release. The Hudson is a blackwater river, with all the underwater visibility of chocolate milk, and a loud one, especially in winter, when snowflakes striking the water's surface set up a high-frequency roar. Human senses miss the snow-thunder entirely, but for eel and sturgeon, the great river is as noisy as Times Square.

Throughout the urban night, New York's 722 miles of subway line stay open, though service slows. Here an A train snakes east through the Jamaica marshes, there a late run noses toward the Columbia campus through its caves of white Inwood marble and gray Fordham gneiss. But the big roadways into the city are nearly deserted at this hour. Tolltakers nod in their booths beside the New York exit ramps of the Garden State Parkway, or the empty E-ZPass lanes flung across the Tappan Zee. Even in Van Cortlandt Park, crossed by three Bronx expressways, the flying squirrels have emerged to dine and socialize, soaring from branch to branch under the municipal moon.

Wall Street Losses

By five in the morning, some nights, the moon is down, sunk beyond the benzene inlets and cyanide pools of the Jersey Meadowlands west of town. The gently radioactive hills of Staten Island, veined with uranium-rich red and green serpentinite, are dwarfed by the dark bulk of the Fresh Kills Landfill at the island's south end, five hundred feet tall, the highest point on the eastern seaboard. In the Staten Island wetlands, feral dogs search for crabs and birds' eggs. A few commercial fishing boats are still moving up the harbor, glimmering belowdecks with bluefish and cod for the city's five thousand restaurants; in urban bakeries from Canarsie to Turtle Bay, the yeast is popping and working in the dough. Though dance clubs and emergency rooms and newsrooms have stayed wakeful, most of New York's eight million humans lie unconscious in their rented burrows, the city's dominant daylight species finally, grudgingly, asleep. Only the skyline blazes.

In the New York financial district, between midnight and dawn, security guards patrolling near the World Trade Center watch the night sky above Manhattan's tip, and listen for birdsong. Billions of migrating birds rush over North America twice a year, seeking breeding grounds and winter homes, heading north with the spring and south in fall. Nearly a hundred species pass directly over Manhattan Island. Some long-distance commuters like to call to each other as they fly: white-throated sparrows heading from Honduras to breeding grounds in Quebec; magnolia warblers making the run from Panama to the Adirondacks. When the seasons are changing, you can stand on Wall Street in the small hours and hear the migrants calling, faint and high, as they stream above the sleeping city. Some travel singly, some in groups: a kettle of hawks, a siege of herons, a wedge of swans. Aerial traffic rises near each equinox, but migrating birds fly over Manhattan nearly every night of the year.

At six in the morning on this raw October Saturday, the financial district is deserted, and cloud wraps the twin corporate towers of the World Trade Center and the World Financial Center from base to crown. "I've brought fresh mealworms," Rebekah Creshkoff assures me, patting a side pocket in her khaki vest as we turn onto a silent Vesey Street. During the work week, Creshkoff tries to carry mealworms in her purse, just in case, but she probably will not use them today. Last night was foggy, and she expects the worst.

"Slink along the walls, so we don't startle anything," Creshkoff warns, scanning a concrete walkway beside the American Express headquarters. False alarm: wet cigar. False alarm: banana peel. First live sighting: a male cardinal perched in a potted yew, looking sleepy and cross. On the dank pavement beyond is a small still form. "Blackpoll," says Creshkoff softly, bending down. "No, black-and-white warbler." She spreads its wings with a fingertip, turns the creamy breast skyward to examine the ebony stippling, and peers at a still-lustrous dark eye. Then she seals the body in a plastic Ziploc bag, scribbles on it the date and place of discovery, and tucks the dead warbler deep in another vest pocket.

Rebekah Creshkoff is fit, pretty, dark-haired, in her thirties; a latecomer birder who grew up in New Jersey, went to Brandeis and Sarah Lawrence, and then (years into a business career) took a birding class on a whim. She liked it enough to enter a Columbia University certification program in conservation biology. Creshkoff knows the financial district's glassy maze by heart because she works here, as a communications officer at the Chase Manhattan Bank. But often she leaves her Upper West Side apartment at 5:45 A.M., biking eight miles down-island to check in with porters and doormen and security patrols, who tell her what they have seen in the night. Manny at the World Trade Center is especially vigilant.

"He's been picking up injured fliers for years," says Creshkoff, waving to a massive bundled figure. "He feels sorry for them. A *big* kid, and such tiny birds." Manny's tips, as always, are to the point. Stunned bird near a brokerage entrance. Dead bird on the Vesey Street sidewalk. Dazed and frantic bird trapped under a glass overhang; seeing a ficus tree in the lobby, it apparently tried to roost but smashed into the building's window wall instead, confused by multiple reflections from wet marble and shadowy panes.

We trace a looping path around the bases of the World Trade Center towers, looking for crash victims. Rats the size of guinea pigs chitter to one another as they search the corporate lawns for injured songbirds to devour.

"I found a scarlet tanager trapped in a revolving door once," says Creshkoff, pointing. "I put it in a vest pocket, called my office to say I had a dentist's appointment, and took it on the subway to Central Park. About halfway uptown it started feeling better and tried to scrabble its way out, as in: 'Is that a scarlet tanager in your pocket, or are you just glad to see me?' It clearly thought, as birds will, 'Oh, my God, she's going to eat me.' "

Liberated at the Fifty-ninth Street entrance to Central Park, the tanager vanished into the treetops. "Did it seem grateful?" I ask. "Do any of them?" Creshkoff shrugs. "Sometimes I think so. It's like kids; they never call, they never write."

When Creshkoff does find stunned birds in the financial district, she coaxes them into a paper bag, carries them to a nearby park, then offers fresh mealworms, and second chances. If she encounters a survivor, she can't keep it; under the federal Migratory Bird Act of 1916, you can be in possession of a live bird for twenty-three hours, but not twenty-five.

Mostly she finds the dead. The bright lights of office towers seem to short-circuit the natural navigational abilities of birds in flight. Sophisticated city breeds like pigeons and sparrows stay calm when they see a city skyline at night. Songbirds travel late, when air currents are calmest, and steer by the stars. But Manhattan buildings can be a quarter-mile high. Migrants see light directly in their flight path, follow it trustingly, then circle the Chrysler Building or the World Trade Center, mesmerized, until exhaustion claims them.

In Toronto, thanks to a special plea by Prince Philip and the World Wildlife Fund, many hotel and office towers now turn off lights during migration season. Chicago has begun a similar program, on a smaller scale. Hearing of the Toronto efforts, Creshkoff wanted to go to Manhattan building managers and ask for their help directly. Better to collect hard evidence, the Canadians told her. So casualties retrieved on Creshkoff's rounds find temporary storage in her apartment freezer. When there's no more room for the Häagen-Dazs, she FedExes a load of frozen birds to researchers at Maryland's Patuxent Avian Research Laboratory. They send her a special cooler; she fills it with skyscraper kill and ships it back; they pay.

"It's hard to imagine New York's commercial landlords voluntarily dimming their lights at night," says Creshkoff gloomily. "If I go to the World Trade towers and say, 'Yo, turn off your lights to save the songbirds,' I look like a lunatic. Though you never know—there's closet birders everywhere." (The Empire State Building's management will sometimes dim its lights in migration season, a welcome exception.)

We slink on, veering toward the brokerages nearer the harbor, checking the overpasses between buildings, the empty sidewalks, and the Winter Garden, whose handsome expanses of lighted glass are a prime deathtrap for birds. Creshkoff points again. Hopping at the edge of a steam grate is a young male common yellowthroat. (A neotropical migrant, my Peterson's field guide notes: summers in Canada, winters in the West Indies. Wrenlike. Four inches long. Plumage a rich yellow shading to olive-brown below. Song: a bright rapid chant, *witchety-witchety-witch*.)

"The yellowthroats are tiny but resilient," says Creshkoff, watching it explore the gutter, head cocked. "More than half will live, once trapped among these buildings. Most songbirds won't."

Dawn is finally here, the chill half-light turning from slate to gray to pearl all around us, the corporate towers vanishing halfway up into sea fog. Creshkoff's early-morning tours have brought all sorts of wild encounters. One spring, she found a live female red-bellied woodpecker, clinging to a polished marble wall; and once a little brown bat huddled on a steel pillar, dazed with cold. She has found a dozen stranded woodcocks, as well as a Virginia rail that wandered the World Trade plaza for nearly a week, subsisting on French fries.

On their worst day ever, Creshkoff and other volunteers have logged sixty-four birds, injured or dead. A good day, always, means capturing survivors and getting them to open space. World Trade victims are usually discovered in the margins and shadows, fatally baffled by stone, steel, and glass. On the Marriott Hotel walkway, we find a black-throated blue warbler with a broken neck; it probably flew to its death trying to reach the reflected trees in the hotel's window wall.

"See the vest-pocket-handkerchief marking on the wing?" says Creshkoff, bagging and noting. "The black-throated blues are extremely vulnerable to collisions with glass. I've never found a live one."

She has had an exhausted hermit thrush fall from the sky at her feet by the Winter Garden; has found an orchard oriole lost on Wall Street; has seen sudden irruptions of species from the boreal forest invade lower Manhattan, then leave just as suddenly—chickadees, winter finches. By 5 World Trade Center, she once taught a wood thrush about glass, tapping and tapping as it fluttered by a window until it finally turned to the real garden instead of the mirage, and lived. She has even pursued an especially stubborn marsh wren around the Chase Manhattan plaza, tossing it mealworms till it overate, got drowsy, and could be moved to safety.

As we cross the barren plazas, looking, looking, knots of homeless men have begun to stand and stretch. The great towers have begun to warm up too, and make small creaks and chirpings as they do, disconcerting to a birder. Soon this plaza will close for the winter, before the annual icefalls can begin. A hard winter in downtown Manhattan sends ice slabs dropping into the World Trade courtyard from a hundred stories up. Halfway across the largest plaza, we spot a white-throated sparrow and a hermit thrush, wandering the concrete reaches in short puzzled flights. "Hurry, guys," Creshkoff pleads. The peregrine falcons who nest on a nearby Wall Street window ledge will soon begin their morning hunt.

The last set of glass walls between fallen migrants and the New Jersey hills is 6 World Trade Center, and in a dim corner we find a white-throated sparrow, several days dead. "My husband says the main difference between us and the birds is that they know they *can* die, while we know we *will* die," says Creshkoff, writing out another label.

From a concrete planter comes a sudden frantic chirring.

"Oh, my God, a winter wren! Jesus Christ! Be careful, boy!" The wren, small, dark, and round, darts down a pillared concourse and is lost to sight, a classic LBJ (little brown job) of a bird. We follow. No sign of the wren, but slumped in a dark corner is a dead female yellowthroat, her body still quite warm, her plumage, even in disarray, as tender and precise as a Dürer watercolor. The yellowthroat's wing feathers ripple for an instant in the Hudson River wind. Sighing, Creshkoff digs for a Ziploc.

"I could put her in an envelope and mail her with one first-class stamp. Feel how light."

Another Wall Street loss. I look up at the great towers with the clouds about their knees, and stroke the honey and amber of the dead breast. If I had not seen the warbler lying in my hand, I would swear my palm was empty.

When historians look at New York, they see an overgrown port town that exists for just one reason: making money. When sociologists look at New York, they perceive two cities, not one, since the workaday outer boroughs have far more in common with Rust Belt capitals like Baltimore or Cleveland than with theatrical, ravenous, self-centered Manhattan. Linguists who come to New York ride the subways and stand on line at coffee shops to construct a taxonomy of urban chat. The city harbors nine distinct dialects of local English, from Old New York (the socialite accent that renders *fur* as "fuh" and *park* as "pahk") to Italian Neighborhood, which pronounces *beard* and *bad* the same way: "bee-ahd." When human geographers look at New York, they see a view-shed, the places where Manhattan's skyline is first visible on the horizon, night and day. Or they map the city's news-shed, within which the New York *Daily News* is the morning's first read and not, say, *The Philadelphia Inquirer.* Or else they trace the New York sports-shed—the zip codes where the Yankees and the Knicks are considered home teams.

Physical geographers studying the metropolitan area prefer to learn its watersheds, the areas of land that drain rainwater and snowmelt into the nearest marsh or lake or stream. Though New York is a strikingly energy-efficient city—mostly because it stacks and packs its residents, then makes them use mass transit—the New York suburbs invented sprawl, and sprawl makes floods, bad ones. Turbodevelopment has erased 90 percent of the New York region's original marshes and meadows, and the replacement fields of asphalt and concrete neatly repel water instead of letting it soak in; any big rainfall must now rush instead to the nearest river, filling basements and subway tunnels on its way to the sea. Forcing eastern rivers into huge cement culverts, Los Angeles–style, is not an option, nor is controlling and rationing every bucket of moisture, as farms and cities along the Colorado try to. Nor can the Northeast use levees or relocation to avert river trouble, as states along the Mississippi used to believe. The New York passion for pavement has warped the work of eleven watersheds in four states, an American record. The metro area is mostly floodplain, but its twenty million residents have nowhere to go, and no one to order it.

For when political scientists look at the New York conurbation, they see one of the great unnatural wonders of the policy world. The New York area is the most elaborate, least manageable civic aggregation in human history, a polycentric supramegalopolis. New York ignores the nation at its back whenever it can. It would like to be a city-state, but in four centuries has devised neither a governing authority nor (unlike New England or southern California) a convincing regional narrative. No one runs New York, not really; power is spread unevenly among some fifteen hundred local governments, districts and authorities, very loosely federated, shifting and shoving for advantage in a thirty-one-county region where some sections are all but deserted for lack of capital and others superheated. With Manhattan's Times Square as its unofficial epicenter, the New York Standard Consolidated Area extends north up the Hudson Valley nearly to West Point, then curves northeast through the glossy suburbs of Westchester County and lower Connecticut. It reaches straight east from the city to gobble half of Long Island, pushes straight west into Pennsylvania's Pocono Mountains, and stretches fifty miles south past the Raritan River and the commuter towns of central Jersey's wealth belt to where the last sod farms of Princeton have been thickly sown with starter mansions, and Greater New York collides at last with MetroPhiladelphia.

In the last fifty years, New York has outgrown at least three tries at definitive labeling. The postwar boom saw it evolve from an industrial-age metropolis into a world capital of culture, finance, and communication whose real peers were London and Paris. By the mid-1950s and early 1960s—New York's Augustan Age—urbanologists declared New York the star of Megalopolis, the six-hundred-mile skein of development from Boston to Washington that still knits the eastern seaboard into one long, thin, supercilious supercity. Now urban scholars have begun to call New York our prime example of the galactic city (a term invented by geographer Peirce Lewis of Pennsylvania State University), a tissue of development so vast that it creates its own order, in a burst of edge cities and technoburbs, allowing residents to bask in the cultural and economic glow of a New York or Los Angeles while ducking its perpetual downtown crises. In the galactic city, suburbs and exurbs no longer push outward from an urban core like rings on a tree. Instead, most expeditions and interactions are suburb-to-suburb; you create your own metropolis, measuring distance in travel time, not in miles from some distinctive central feature like Times Square or the Loop. Everyone's galactic-city map is different: the favored supermarket is ten minutes away, the preferred mall thirty minutes in another direction, the workplace forty minutes distant—urbanism à la carte.

Yet New York is also a megacity, the urban form whose global fate will shape twenty-first-century life. In 1900, only 14 percent of human beings called a city home, and just eleven places around the world had populations of one million or more. Today, four hundred cities have passed the million mark. In the 1970s, New York, London, Tokyo, and Los Angeles emerged as the world's first four megacities, defined (then and now) as urban areas whose population is over ten million, and climbing. By 1995, the megacity count had risen to fourteen.

North American members were Mexico City, New York, Los Angeles, and (just barely) Toronto. Chicago is too small still for megacity status, even though its metro area spans four states and covers an area roughly the size of New Jersey. The year 2015 will see twenty-six megacities, all of them in the developing world except for New York, Los Angeles, London, Toronto, Tokyo, and Osaka: think Lagos and Dacca, São Paulo and Rio de Janiero, Bombay and Beijing. Most residents of megacities already live—or fail to—on less than one dollar a day. In the year 2000, Earth's human population is six billion; by 2030, the United Nations warns, megacity slums alone will contain that many and more.

But to an ecologist, New York is most interesting as an ecotone, a place where natural worlds collide—northern and southern climate zones overlapping, land melting into ocean, saltwater mixing with fresh. Six natural habitats define the city of New York: estuary, salt marsh, woodland, beach, freshwater river, and prairie. Some of these ecosystems are relics now, like the improbable patch of virgin forest in upper Manhattan's Inwood Hill Park, and some are remakes, like the re-created Eastern grassland at Brooklyn's old Floyd Bennett Airfield. Centuries of human assault on New York's natural underpinnings have fragmented and degraded all the city's original habitats, sky and water, leaf and stone. Ecologists, in their off-duty hours, abandon algorithms of species loss and formulas of oxygenation and call the problem by its street name: creeping crud.

The earth scientists, especially, believe you cannot know a place without ground-truthing it. One walks a piece of ground, or flies low over it, or rows the waters around it, taking time to *see* as well as look, rather than trusting what tradition says is there, or what theory tells you should be. Manhattan is indeed the world's most densely developed real estate, as New York and its outliers are the very paradigm of sprawl. But even in the ultimate city—*especially* in the ultimate city—what you see depends on where you stand. Chicago is an ex-swamp, with one wild edge: the inland freshwater sea of Lake Michigan. Los Angeles is a desert temporarily disguised, with two wild edges: the Pacific Ocean and the San Gabriel Mountains. In New York, hardwood forest marks the city's north rim, from Far Hills over to New Caanan; the swampy Meadowlands, thirty-two square miles of phragmites, cordgrass, and salt hay, form the city's western barrier; and to the south and east is New York's deepwater face, 580 miles of shoreline within city limits, particularly where the Hudson estuary widens into a superb natural harbor, then merges with the Atlantic beyond Fire Island. (On its southwest side, the city fronts New Jersey, which is attached to the mainland only by a fifty-mile strip of land at its crown. Otherwise, the Garden State lies afloat off the eastern seaboard, the Delaware River defining one border and the Jersey Shore the other.)

So: a megacity with three wild edges—forest, marsh, and sea. But a second New York ground-truth is the sheer amount of open land within city limits. One-quarter of New York is open space. It has more than twenty-eight thousand acres of parkland, five hundred acres of mudflat and wetland, five thousand acres of serious forest. Anyone can get lost in the woods in New York, and every month dozens of locals and tourists do, guided back to pavement by the Parks Department's patient urban rangers, or the NYPD.

All five New York boroughs retain places where you can

walk for hours and see no other human near. Northern Manhattan has its lonely salt marshes; the Staten Island greenbelt, three times the size of Central Park, shelters spring-fed kettle ponds and dwarf-pine forests. At Wave Hill in the Bronx, in fall, you can see broad-winged hawks crossing the Hudson at the rate of a thousand a day. Brooklyn is gentle prairie by the bay, punctuated by an abandoned control tower, supports 140 acres of wildflowers and big bluestem, a scene straight out of Kansas. Beside New York's largest airport, JFK International, lies the Jamaica Bay Wildlife Refuge, some parts all marsh, others sand and cactus. Snowy owls come to Jamaica Bay when the weather turns cold, eager to hunt rats and rabbits along the runways next door. The level winterscape of the great airport apparently reminds them of their native tundra in Siberia and Baffin Bay. Whole clans of snowy owls now fly down from the Arctic each year to winter in Queens.

When a snowy owl looks at New York, it sees safety. And lunch. And a frontier. A great many birds and animals are discovering that city living can be less stressful than a career in the wild. Natural time scales may differ from ours, but nature's agenda never changes. It will take over, if it can. New York is a fine place to start. Ecologists know that big cities are far more friendly to wildlife than small ones, because the potential habitat is both immense and varied. Parks and greenways and suburban gardens offer ideal hiding places and travel corridors; urban creeks and backyard lap pools and corporate fountains yield reliable fresh water. To a twenty-first-century raccoon or deer, New York (or Atlanta, or Frankfurt) looks like a fine big animal sanctuary, with the prime food sources in the middle of town.

Sometimes the incoming species are only taking over the

parts of the city that we avoid. Of the nation's twenty-five largest cities in 1950, eighteen had lost population to the burbs by 2000, the vertical city succeeded by the horizontal city. Urban researchers call it the paradox of the green ghetto, best seen in depopulating urban settings, like the modern ruins of downtown Detroit, where pheasants fly over the aging freeways; or East St. Louis, where weeds cover railroad tracks and the basics of city life—a corner store, a taxicab, a fire department—are rare sightings; or north Philadelphia, where small trees have begun to grow in the streets. New York is unusual because it still has a lively downtown (Manhattan's lower half) making it one of very few United States cities with both a vital heart and an active edge. But overall, the American city in the last fifty years has become more crowded and voracious at the margins, quieter and greener and wilder at the core. If desolate sections and marginal neighborhoods are rehabilitated and rediscovered, plant and animal resettlers tend to stay. The urban world is not particularly easy on the so-called equilibrium species, like trees, which tend to develop and reproduce slowly, grow large, and prefer stable environments, but it can be much kinder than country existence for short-lived opportunists like mice or milkweed, which live on the margins and must be quick to exploit ephemera: a sunny vacant lot, a cache of seed, a baseboard hole. And for predators, like sharks or falcons or viruses, the New York hunting is, as ever, sublime.

The Falcon's Map

In the decorous, expensive East Sixties, between York Avenue and the East River, New York Hospital and Cornell Medical Center share a tall Depression Gothic clinic of glazed white brick, four blocks long and streamlined like a Hupmobile. Above its Sixty-eighth Street entrance, a full May moon is fading in the periwinkle sky. Through the hum of early traffic on the FDR Drive, I hear a peregrine falcon's homecoming cry, as it circles in from Astoria and Forest Hills: a high, unearthly *hwee, hwee.*

Christopher Nadareski, a wildlife biologist in his late thirties, sturdy and bearded, waits by the express elevator, wearing a padded navy snowmobile suit and holding high a stout wooden stake. "Vampires pretty bad today, huh?" says a passing resident in scrubs.

It is 6:10 A.M. Nadareski has just over an hour to inspect a brood of peregrine falcon chicks before the hospital day begins. He has worked for the New York City Department of Environmental Protection since earning his master's degree in wildlife management from the State University of New York at New Paltz, and this is his eleventh banding trip to New York/Cornell, one of the city's most successful peregrine nest sites, and possibly its most inconvenient. The hospital's breeding pair has chosen to live in a plywood nest box anchored to a wind-battered cornice on the twenty-seventh floor, just outside the AIDS clinic.

Working fast, Nadareski and an assistant spread falcon-tending tools on a hospital gurney. O-ring spreaders. Leather gauntlets. A chime of metal leg bands: one set alphanumeric, another the black U.S. Fish and Wildlife Service crimp bands used for all migratory birds. Last comes a white motorcycle helmet, severely scratched.

"I've banded many, many falcons, and believe me, they remember the helmet," says Nadareski, wedging open the aged sash window with his wooden stake. "Each time I'm here, the doctors get to apply medical aid. When you crawl out on the ledge, their line of attack is direct—your head, your right arm, your ear. They really like my ear. They see flesh, that's *it*."

The eastward view from the clinic tower is formidable— traffic helicopters dart past at eye level, and morning mist fills the little valleys of upper Queens—but Nadareski has yet to appreciate it. To retrieve chicks from the nest box, he must crawl out a nursing-office window and slide along a ten-inch stone ledge, three hundred feet above the parking lot, net in hand. Young peregrines are born mostly naked and sprout white down within days, staying in the nest about six weeks before beginning to fly, or trying to. Only one urban chick in three survives fledging from a bridge; two in three will survive the initial attempt to launch from a building. (A New York/Cornell fledgling once managed to fall thirty stories down a hospital smokestack, but was discovered and saved by a maintenance crew.)

Though *peregrine* comes from the Latin for "wanderer," a good part of any falcon's day is spent immobile on some high viewpoint, staring. "Playing statue," Nadareski calls it. Falcons are famously undomestic: they prefer good views to comfort, and in the wild will merely scratch themselves a crude cliffside hollow for sleeping and breeding, called an eyrie. As late as the 1940s, peregrines lived on Central Park West and on the roof of the fashionable St. Regis Hotel, just off Fifth Avenue, but by 1970 the pesticide DDT had made the peregrine falcon an endangered species and, in the Northeast, an extinct one. Barely three hundred pairs survived nationwide. But between 1974 and 1988, the Peregrine Fund and the New York State Department of Environmental Conservation released more than one hundred young peregrines in New York State—up in the Adirondacks and in the city of New York itself. In 1983, after an absence of nearly thirty years, one peregrine pair successfully nested on the underside of the Verrazano-Narrows Bridge, while a second found a home on the Throgs Neck span.

Baltimore, Seattle, Boston, Los Angeles, Milwaukee, and Chicago now support urban falcons too, but the New York region boasts more breeding pairs than any city in the world— four nest sites on buildings and eight on bridges, or about 10 percent of the eastern United States peregrine population. Ambitious young peregrines come to New York from as far away as Virginia and Maine in search of big-city mates, and big-city hunting and fighting. Mock duels are not the falcon way. When peregrines struggle for territory, there are no draws and no rematches. The loser either dies or is promptly forced out of town in disgrace, to Long Island or New Jersey. (Peregrine battles in the urban canyons have converted any number of market traders and account executives into nine-to-five birders, one population of top predators saluting another.)

A smash, a scream, another smash. Nadareski's white helmet has done its work. Before he is halfway out the clinic window, first the female peregrine, then the male, flies straight at the pane just above him, raking the glass with talons and beak to frighten off this dawn intruder. As Nadareski crawls toward the plywood nest box, both parents circle the hospital tower, diving repeatedly and screaming as they dive.

"It's PJ!" says a watching staff physician, delighted to see an old friend. "Clean breast, seems to be in nice shape, though—yes—I see a bit of blood on his beak. More than a bit."

Even for a peregrine, PJ is aggressive, but his mate is more so; male peregrines, sometimes called tiercels, are one-third smaller than the females, who measure twenty inches from head to tail, about the size of a crow. Falcondom is a matriarchy. The female assumes the lead when hunting in pairs, takes on the largest prey, and eats first. The original peregrine staple was the passenger pigeon, but New York's two million modern pigeons have proven an excellent substitute, if supplemented with starlings, blue jays, and the occasional bat. Adult peregrines are slate-colored, their backs and wings gray-blue, with white chests and underwings flecked in deeper gray. Dark face stripes disguise the movement of their eyes when watching quarry. They are the swiftest creatures on Earth, able to dive at 200 miles an hour. The New York falcons, however, have adapted to local conditions by perfecting a video-game hunting style, curving and weaving at high speed among tall buildings, instead of plummeting straight down as they would in more open country.

Some New York peregrines decide on tower life, like the young New York/Cornell male who found a starter aerie in the carillon of Riverside Church, across the street from Grant's Tomb in upper Manhattan. (Discovering chunks of fresh jay on his front sidewalk, Riverside's building manager looked up— way up—saw falcons among the gargoyles, and called Nadareski.) Other peregrines take to the bridges: the Throgs Neck, Tappan Zee, Verrazano-Narrows, and George Washington spans all shelter falcon families now. A pair hunts pigeons and blue jays about the grounds of the New York Public Library. Another lives on a tower of the Brooklyn Bridge, unbanded, since the New York City fire department and the Department of Transportation can't agree on how to get Nadareski within netting distance.

Outside the clinic window the parents' threats redouble— *keekkeekkeekKEEK*—and both birds attack in earnest, beating on the white helmet, ripping at Nadareski's arm and neck as he edges toward safety with a female chick in his net. Her downy plumage is the the bright opaque white of bond paper. The pale-yellow feet, three-toed and furiously kicking, look far too large for her robin-sized body. She smells like pepper and hay. Nadareski lowers the falcon chick into a gray plastic box, where she remains flat on her back, panting in shock, a tiny peach-colored tongue pulsing within the gaping half-inch beak. Her eyes are dark brown, with wide black pupils and a pale blue rim. "Hey, no bugs," says the assistant biologist, checking nape and belly for bird lice. Another fledgling slides into the examination box, wings spread high; a third backs slowly into one corner, slowly stamping both feet to intimidate the clutch of humans looming above and making distinctive species sounds: "So cute!" "Look at those little bitty toes!"

In managing the world's largest metropolitan-falcon program, Nadareski has two ongoing headaches: the tremendous annual death rate among fledglings and the tremendous turnover among building and maintenance staff at the dozen nesting sites ("Falcons? Here? What falcons?"). The reeducation cycle is endless. New Yorkers who do know about the peregrines often want to treat them as taxpayer pets, not wild birds. Disturbance at nesting sites is rising, a problem nearly as intractable as the politics of wildlife, local, state, and federal. Yet Nadareski also encounters New Yorkers without agendas: tough bridge guys who rescue wailing chicks from girders; building superintendents determined to guard the peregrines' privacy; retirees with good binoculars who log falcon activity minute by minute; Wall Street office workers who hold contests to name the birds, and raffles to help them. (In some United States cities, like Seattle and Rochester, the local peregrines have their own Internet Web site, featuring live candid shots from a hidden nest cam. New York peregrines have their own publicist, courtesy of the city's Department of Environmental Protection.)

Falcons rule the New York air life, the city aspect locals most often miss. Only out-of-towners are uncool enough to stare up in public, which is why visitors and not natives usually spot the monarch butterflies along Fifth Avenue, some drifting just feet above the oblivious crowds, others thirty floors high. Every fall, millions of orange-and-black migrants pass through the city, heading for winter homes in the Mexican mountains.

Plein air New York is famously strange. The city has five individual weather systems, one per borough; a single storm over the city can mean drizzle in Central Park but a cloudburst in Bensonhurst, since Queens and southern Brooklyn nearly always get the strongest thunderstorms and heaviest rains. Brooklyn is the coldest borough, Queens the warmest, the Bronx the snowiest, Staten Island the wettest. Manhattan has the best urban whirlwinds (especially along Sixth Avenue at midtown) but the fewest rainbows; air pollution obscures the refracted colors, and too many buildings crowd out the dome of sky. New York even makes its own rainy weekends, since carbon monoxide from traffic plus long-distance pollutants from superstacks along the Great Lakes often trigger rainclouds by the workweek's end. Quieter Sundays clean the air before the cycle starts again, though not without casualties: the Statue of Liberty loses a pound of copper each year thanks to acid rain. In September and October, tiny white particles sometimes shower midtown, and anxious calls deluge the city's Environmental Protection Agency: Is it asbestos? Is it ash? Is it nuclear fallout? It's dandelion fluff, say the patient EPA operators: when the autumn winds are strong, ripe seeds from Central Park and Flushing Meadow swirl over Manhattan, ready to colonize pastures a hundred years gone.

All this information shapes the falcon's map of New York, which is highly balkanized and changeable, a dozen pigeon-rich territories carved in air. Unlike the Saul Steinberg rendering of New York as New Yorkers see it—Manhattan obsessively foregrounded, the boroughs as bridge-and-tunnel provinces, and anything past Paramus a study in rattlesnakes and polyester— a falcon's cartography is starkly strategic. The peregrines of

48 Wall Street have moved to 55 Water Street, just around the corner, but continue to patrol the financial district east of Broadway. The falcons of the Verrazano-Narrows Bridge control all aerial passage from Brooklyn to Staten Island. Those based on the Queens tower of the Throgs Neck Bridge rule south of the Cross Island Parkway, while the New York/Cornell pair supervise the Upper East Side and much of Queens. The falcons of Riverside Church are perhaps the city's busiest, since they must watch over Riverside Park, monitor the rich Hudson River bird traffic, *and* defend a long swath of Manhattan's West Side, from Zabar's up to Washington Heights, where falcon fancier John James Audubon is buried.

Naturalists call falcons a charismatic species. Megafauna like eagles and tigers and bears and great white sharks are charismatic species too, the celebs and tycoons of the wild world, glamorous and deadly. Edge species, however, are the risk-takers and fast adapters, suited to life in disturbed places, or poor soil, or both: abandoned factories, brownfields, vacant lots, old rail corridors. Sparrows and gingko trees are edge species, like raccoons and deer, like first-generation immigrants. Exurbs and strip malls and office parks are all edge species. Keystone species are the patient workhorses of creation, easy to overlook the first time around. Oak trees and plankton, firefighters and nurses, are keystones, and so are Flatbush and Far Rockaway. Indicator species serve as guides to an area's health. In a South Florida swamp, panthers and osprey are indicator species, their return signaling a recovering ecosystem; in the Arctic, if the polar bears are healthy, then the local food web is probably lively too, good news for the region's other residents, from seals to microbes. Professional citywatchers often gauge the vigor of a

New York borough by its urban indicator species: free-spending tourists, middle-class families, realtors with Palm Pilots.

Sentinel species are our early-warning system, quick to perceive environmental imbalance, quick to suffer its less happy effects. Songbirds are a good sentinel species. Their numbers have begun to fluctuate for no clear reason, and researchers are asking why: pollution? disease? tower-kill? Or is development logging their tropical winter refuges and paving over their northern breeding grounds? Frogs are sentinels too. Their delicate permeable skins—unprotected, like ours—are exquisitely vulnerable to environmental stressors, like pesticides, solvents, parasites, climate change, or ultraviolet seepage through a thinning ozone layer. When amphibians start to develop strange tumors, or hatch with legs missing and eyes askew, or die off with no clear cause, researchers start to wonder if the worldwide frog slump is only another boom-and-bust population cycle of the sort nature does so well, or a firebell in the night.

Professional observers and rememberers who witness and wait, from urban historians to field scientists, are sentinels too. So is New York. For centuries now, New York has been the bellwether of United States cities, the place where the future shows up first. Los Angeles is our classic anticity; Chicago the last functioning industrial-age metropolis, an urban coelacanth; Atlanta, Houston, and Phoenix the avatars of sprawl; Miami the link to the other Americas. But New York is the miner's canary of American city life. As it goes, so goes the nation—and, often, the world.

Bearing a last complaining chick, Nadareski descends the ladder once more, trying not to disturb the bound epidemiology journals and flow charts of protease inhibitors. "Do you like heights?" I ask. "I notice you don't use a rope." He grimaces. "It's better if you don't think about it. I have to trust my own concentration. What I *really* hate are amusement park rides."

Both Nadareski's padded suit and the shirt beneath are badly falcon-ripped, but there is no time to change. Both biologists go swiftly to work, checking each bird's eyes, cloaca, wings, and beak. All are healthy, and they each weigh under a pound: three females and one male. Chick number one remains frozen with fear, letting the humans handle, band, and weigh her without comment or complaint. Number two is a screamer, but Nadareski hoods her gently with a leather glove, holding his palm just above her face to cut down excess stimulation, and she quiets. Number three, the male, tries for cold poise, then flaps a stubby tail and begins to yell. A tooth is developing already in his upper mandible; if he survives, he will soon learn to use it to sever the neck of prey in midair.

Chick four stares at her leg, now sheathed in contrasting metal bands, bird size 7A, then searches the tiled hallway for an escape route. Though barely four weeks old, her samurai nature is fully formed: the hot yellow feet instantly clench and hold anything within range—a sleeve, a finger, a pen—and the blue-rimmed eyes roll round to meet mine, enraged. We have interrupted her breakfast (Central Park starling and blue jay, according to the debris sample Nadareski has taken from the nest) and she is not pleased.

Cupped between my palms, the young bird pushes both wings strongly out and in, out and in, no panicked beating, only a twelve-ounce predator's imperious demand: release me, or I will kill you. She throws back her head and screams, the long shrill hunting cry. It is 7:30 A.M. Nadareski rises to begin returning the banded chicks to their nest box. Diving through the blue and gold morning light, the adult falcons continue to smash headlong at the tall east window, still tearing at the glass with beaks and claws. The agitated nestling begins to shed. Silver down fills the clinic air like spring snow.

Unleashed

When Christopher Nadareski finishes banding falcon chicks on the Upper East Side, he often drives directly to one of New York City's nineteen water reservoirs, carrying a boom box in the back of his white state-issued van. Moving people over and under water is a New York specialty: the city has twenty tunnels and seventy-six bridges, from the Hell Gate, the Lemon Creek, and the Throgs Neck to the Triborough and the Brooklyn. But getting fresh water to New York's people has always been a problem. The wells of Manhattan Island were already brackish and overstrained when Aaron Burr and Alexander Hamilton launched the ingenious scam called the Manhattan Water Company (which never delivered the cheap potable water it promised, but did eventually become the Chase Manhattan Bank).

For a city where something is always blowing up or burning down, no reliable clean-water supply meant smallpox, yellow fever, cholera, and block-devouring fires until the 1840s. But then an earthen reservoir, slope-sided like an Egyptian mastaba, was finally built at the corner of Forty-second and Fifth, where the New York Public Library stands today, and by 1910 the city's drinking water was being piped in from the Catskill Mountains, north and west of the city. Except for some wells in Brooklyn and Queens, it still is. More than three hundred miles of aqueduct bring New Yorkers 1.5 billion gallons a day of potable water (which means water strenuously doused with copper sulfate and chlorine, to counter the agricultural runoff, commuter-train oil, airport grime, landfill sludge, and animal droppings picked up en route). Sixty-two hundred miles of sewers carry away over a billion gallons of urban wastewater, though the city's rivers and sewer system, as always, remain intimately related, especially on rainy days, when the aged pipes and pools overflow, displacing millions of gallons of sludge and sewage. Should you fall into the East River when it rains, Manhattan hospitals know just what to do: revive patient, call the infectious-diseases team, administer massive doses of antibiotic.

For all its surface dash and glitter, New York is a town of peeling paint, falling masonry, and cracking bridges. Comptrollers say the boroughs need $90 billion in urgent repairs they cannot possibly afford, which is why, six hundred times a year, some arthritic joint in New York's six thousand miles of water pipe will crack and burst, creating a sudden hip-deep street flood, or a bus-eating sinkhole, or a gas-main blast that snaps a fireball six stories high. WHAT NEXT: LOCUSTS? the tabloid headlines inquire.

The watersheds that make New York possible were chosen, in 1870, for their mountain remoteness. But intense development has brought clear-cutting, subdivisions, road runoff, septic tanks—and geese. Nearly all the city's reservoirs are overrun by thousands of Canada geese that have decided migration is a bore. Since just fifty geese can produce 2.5 tons of bacteria-laden droppings a year, state biologists like Christopher Nada-reski climb into elderly motorboats month after month and circle reservoir shorelines, playing tapes of bird-distress calls at high volume, trying to make the flocks nervous enough to move to someone else's watershed. Save one species, repel another. But migration is hard work. The geese don't *want* to commute anymore. They want to dine on succulent golf-course grass and take light exercise in corporate-park ponds, to day-trade, to find their inner gosling. Some Canada geese still migrate the old-fashioned way, in crisply organized arrowhead formations led by the senior females. But millions more have become year-round squatters in towns and cities east of the Mississippi, un-reformable because they no longer know the aerial routes to Ontario or the Carolinas. The chain of memory, once broken, is nearly impossible to repair; they have forgotten all the land-marks, and all the journey-cries.

Calling such geese sky carp, pond starlings, or flying rats doesn't help, though playing hiphop near them often will—geese loathe hiphop—and renting a hit squad of border collies, trained to goose-herd, can be useful too. Some cities send out workers to shake goose eggs in order to addle them, or to coat eggs in mineral oil, which prevents hatching. Controlling big citified birds is an uncertain, labor-intensive art. In Portland, Oregon, bald eagles battle and breed in downtown pockets of green; in Seattle, hungry eagles cruise the Woodland Park Zoo (terrifying the tame zoo birds), then dive-bomb local ponds to carry off ducklings. In the Los Angeles suburbs of Palos Verdes and Arcadia, flocks of peremptory feral peacocks (long-ago es-capees from a local arboretum) regularly snarl traffic and soil lawns. On Martha's Vineyard, foraging wild turkeys chase senior citizens, peck the paint off car doors, and walk through open sliding doors to root through sofa cushions in search of stray Cheerios. Island football fans and funeral processions alike have learned to proceed on turkey time; a sixty-bird flock can hold up a lot of cars.

An urban retaking can assume many forms, and find many routes. Central Park's wild turkey apparently arrived by flying from the Bronx straight down Broadway late at night, then making a left near Lincoln Center. Porpoises are exploring the Hudson again, playing near the Williamsburg Bridge, then heading upriver. Snapping turtles seem to be using the Cross Bay Bridge for their migrations, say startled herpetologists at the Jamaica Bay Wildlife Refuge, or else they somehow manage to cross two busy Queens highways; only the turtles know. (Some New York turtles have been recently fitted with tiny radio transmitters, to satisfy human curiosity.) When coyotes want to see New York, they use the Major Deegan Expressway, and often get run over in the process. The city Parks Department would like to see COYOTE CROSSING signs on assorted Bronx arteries, to keep New York drivers alert; the Bronx has a growing coyote pack, migrants from neighboring Westchester.

After several rewarding days of Dumpster-diving, a black bear was recently captured on a golf course in the Westchester suburb of White Plains, not far from the local branch of Bloomingdale's. On a wild diet, black bears produce one or two cubs, but scavenging our leftovers provides enough calories to produce three or four a year. Fast food creates jumbo-size bears— six hundred pounds versus the more usual three hundred. Twentieth-century bears used to get hit by cars; now, their larger, stronger, less fearful descendants show each other how to rip open a Toyota like a can of beans. Raccoons, even smarter and more adaptable, have recolonized parks and sewers in every New York borough. Some wildlife biologists suspect they never left. Raccoons have been seen teaching their kits to look both ways before crossing Manhattan streets; they squeeze through cat doors in Queens neighborhoods to raid kitchen refrigerators; they make lavish dens in attics all over town. Nearly every day, city animal-control officers pull protesting coons from cozy nests of pink insulation and deport them upstate.

But the most dangerous animal in North America remains the white-tailed deer. Deer persistently roam the runways at Philadelphia International; at Dulles, a deer jumped through a window in the main terminal and ran down an up escalator before being subdued at baggage claim. In rutting season, they turn so active and singleminded that the New York State Thruway has added a new alert for motorists to its electronic warning signs: ATTACK DEER. It's barely a joke: the United States deer population has exceeded twenty million. Deer racing through traffic cause accidents that injure or kill more than thirty thousand humans a year, and require a billion dollars in auto repairs.

Far too many American deer are suburbanites. Suburban development typically leaves a chopped and changed and simplified landscape, a mosaic of fragmented habitats: a subdivision next to a small woodlot, a golf course beside a mall beside an old farm. From coast to coast, good deer habitat has been transformed into ideal deer habitat, a surfeit of edges. Deer charge through playgrounds full of children, steal bedding plants off tailgates, and adroitly jump eight-foot deer fences to find the fifteen pounds of foliage each deer needs each day to survive. In their spare time, deer strip the remaining forest understory, damaging habitat for ground birds like quail and altering tree and plant succession for the worse. Some towns round up their deer and ship them out of state; others choose hired sharpshooters and culling over mass starvation and disease. When the National Park Service tried shooting deer on the Gettysburg battlefield, on the grounds that deer-browsing had damaged historically significant woodlands, animal rights groups halted the hunt by suing in federal court. But since the late 1990s, the urban deer hunt, staged in metropolitan parks and neighborhoods, has become an autumn staple in and around Cleveland, Cincinnati, Minneapolis, Milwaukee, Cedar Rapids, Saint Louis, Kansas City, Pittsburgh, Boston, Chicago, and Washington, D.C. Deer that make it to Manhattan are shot with tranquilizers and deported to New Jersey, though environmental historians murmur that for authenticity's sake, the city should probably reintroduce that most efficient method of deer control, the hungry wolf pack.

If natural New York is back in ways unimaginable in 1900, or 1950, or even 1980, state and federal tries at environmental cleanup are a major reason why. When Congress passed the Clean Air Act in 1970, New York air quality was at its nadir— white gloves would be soot-covered in an hour, and in summer you could stand at St. Patrick's Cathedral, look north to find Central Park, just sixteen blocks away, and see only yellow-gray haze. Midtown air is noticeably clearer now, though the New York region still breathes a carcinogenic bouillabaisse of vinyl chloride, lead, chromium, formaldehyde, and butadiene, plus extreme particulate pollution from diesel trucks, which means that New York still has some of the nation's worst air, along with Houston, Philadelphia, the Los Angeles basin, Salt Lake City, and Phoenix.

When the Nixon administration put through the Clean Water Act in 1972, only one-third of the nation's waterways were fit for human contact, and the Hudson River waters off Manhattan had bacteria counts more than fifty times the safe level for swimming. By 2000, two-thirds of American waters were surprisingly clean. You can actually take a dip in the Hudson, if you're quick about it, and have all your shots. Fishing there remains a calculated urban risk, like falling asleep in Manhattan's Port Authority bus terminal, since the river retains high levels of dioxin and mercury and PCBs, but catch-and-release during a Wall Street lunch hour is a new metropolitan reality. The slowly improving Hudson is one of very few rivers in Europe or North America to sustain spawning runs of all its historic fishes, from shad and sturgeon to tomcod and winter flounder. The signature quarry of river and harbor is the striped bass, known to environmentalists and developers as the fish that stopped Manhattan's habitat-wrecking West Side Highway project a generation back (New York's version of the spotted owl). Marine biologists admire the stripers' taste in real estate, since most of the city's bass winter along the Upper West Side and summer off the Hamptons. Fishing New Yorkers know them as fighters and as urban realists. Silvery, sleek, and muscular, striped bass love to hunt by sewage outfalls, enjoy bumping and harassing commercial divers, and weigh anywhere from twenty to sixty pounds, very unlike the sad New York stripers of the middle twentieth century, enfeebled by tumors, crippled by fin rot, and crusted with toxic slime.

The blue crab and fiddler crab populations are up too, scuttling in their millions along the silty floor of a reoxygenating harbor and estuary; these, in turn, attract thousands of long-legged wading birds. Yellow-crowned night heron, glossy ibis, and great egret are resettling New York's harbor islands, from tiny U Thant Island behind the United Nations Building, with its two trees, to Brooklyn's remote and rocky Swinburne. Their quiet reclamation of former territories has succeeded largely because the harbor acts as a giant moat, keeping human and raccoon predators at bay, and dinner nearby. Many of the great birds are ninth- or tenth-generation New Yorkers now, and to them a harborscape of sunken Chevys and abandoned factories seems entirely proper.

In the twenty-first century, Americans will be dealing not only with a wilder New York but with a wilder East, a wilder South, a wilder Midwest. In all these regions, forests have quietly expanded in the last hundred years, taking back abandoned cropland and old logging tracts; the nineteenth century was far harder on American woodlands even than the twentieth. The return of the eastern forests has been most dramatic of all. Forests arose once more from Maine to Virginia—less impressive than the original, to be sure, and full of cellar holes and barn ruins, mute monuments to what historians call the 80-10-80 effect: an east-of-the-Mississippi landscape with 80 percent tree cover in 1800, stripped down to just 10 percent forest in 1900, that is again 80 percent woodland in 2000. It's definitely second-growth forest, part manipulated and part unplanned, displaying less variety, less interaction, and more scrubby understory than the noble first-growth tracts of Colonial days, where two-hundred-foot elms and chestnuts rose above a parklike woodland floor.

For forest fanciers and forest historians, this latest greening of the East is cubic zirconium instead of immortal diamond. But no ecosystem is immortal, or immutable. The twentieth-century forests were cover, and green, and largely ignored in the city-dazzled industrial age, and safe, since the big predators that ruled them once, like bear and wolves, were long since hunted out. Most of all, the twentieth-century regreening of America's eastern half let animal populations recover—too well, perhaps, since Northeast habitat has again reached capacity. The timing could not be worse. In the first years of the twenty-first century, even these secondhand forests are receding yet again, overwhelmed partly by industrial forestry and partly by development. Two population explosions, human and animal, one terrain. Some species retreat, following their shrinking habitat. Others move to town, or try to.

Across the United States, Department of Agriculture files and state wildlife bureau reports map the resulting confrontations. Along the northern reaches of I-95, the main East Coast interstate corridor, car-moose collisions are a constant danger, thanks largely to timber companies and their clear-cuts, which create vast moose pastures of young trees and help the population thrive. Moose weigh nearly a ton, and usually win in any auto confrontation, except for the one that took up residence in the median strip of Route 128, Boston's high-tech center, and had to be shot by police. Their western cousin, the eight-hundred-pound elk, has begun plodding through suburban neighborhoods in Utah and Colorado, coming down from the Rockies and mixing with humans for the first time in more than a century, though rarely by choice. ("Prime condo habitat is also prime elk habitat," observes the Colorado Department of

Wildlife.) Bewildered herds of cinnamon-brown javelina, looking for the desert acres that were theirs just months before, wander fire-new Tucson subdivisions or planned communities like Anthem, north of Phoenix, a city of fifty thousand people created ex nihilo in 1998; in Anthem's first seven days, the developer sold one thousand house lots. In central Arizona's Prescott Valley, antelope used to run just as freely well into the 1990s, but development has fenced and bulldozed their former grasslands. The surviving antelope graze on the lawn of the Prescott sheriff's department, a doomed urban herd. Bighorn sheep are facing a similar fate in the mountains around Palm Springs, as the Coachella Valley's hundred golf courses and their planned communities push ceaselessly into the foothills, drastically compressing the bighorn's traditional range.

But coyote and vultures are easing into urban areas throughout the lower forty-eight. Nutria, orange-toothed and relentless, are eating their way through urban and suburban wetlands from the Chesapeake to Louisiana. Backyard waterways near Seattle host more and more pods of carnivorous black-and-white orcas—the twenty-foot members of the dolphin family that we call killer whales. Bobcats are back in southern New Jersey's Pine Barrens, much to the surprise of biologists, who decades ago declared them extinct. Along the Mexico-Arizona border, jaguars have resettled their nineteenth-century lands, coming back into the United States to harass livestock, then deciding to stay; jaguars need no green cards.

In Florida, alligators increasingly show up in parking lots, front yards, and golf-course water hazards. Alligators are tough: they will live and breed in drainage ditches, and are not fussy about meals. Far more interesting to wildlife experts is the reappearance of the much choosier native crocodile, once abundant but now shy and rare, whose native mangroves and marshes have been all but erased by a tide of swimming pools and patios. After several difficult decades, when their numbers fell to only a few hundred, American saltwater crocodiles are claiming a new home in the cooling canals of Florida's nuclear power plants, and breeding there at four times the normal rate. Owls are moving into suburbs everywhere, drawn by the easy supply of chihuahuas, schnauzers, and house cats; a great horned owl has a six-foot wingspan, and can easily make off with a twelve-pound pet. From Maine to New Jersey, black bear break into exurban houses, hunting sticks of butter, packs of bratwurst, and rolls of cookie dough. Beaver have re-colonized Boston, Denver, and Dallas, where their urge to re-landscape frequently results in blocked trout streams and threatened septic systems. In Chicago, an urban beaver gnawed down a tree in Grant Park and caused a massive traffic tie-up on Lake Shore Drive; near the Jefferson Memorial in Washington, D.C., a covey of beavers felled a dozen of the famous Japanese cherry trees in a valiant attempt to dam the Tidal Basin.

As the continent's dominant species, we tend to forget how closely other creatures observe our works and days: our high-speed roads, our mystifying preference for sunlight, our delectable garbage. In southern California, mountain lions have been discovered cooling off in garden sprinklers, breaking into houses near Disneyland, investigating Montecito shopping malls, and padding through a Roseville apartment complex built astride a natural pathway between canyons long favored by puma; no one thought to check the natural history of the area before forcing development deep into the foothills. Lion attacks on hikers and joggers from California to Colorado have sharply increased. Generations of big cats have now been born within sight of urban streetlights and highways, especially near the big western cities, and biologists speculate that familiarity has bred such contempt that pumas now consider humans a legitimate part of the food chain.

In the last two decades, the mountain lions of the American West have radically changed schedules and diets, particularly near Yuppified towns like Boulder, Missoula, Sun Valley, and Taos, where they raid pet breakfasts with aplomb (mammologists studying lion scat find lots of Alpo and Purina) and hunt hikers at the previously unheard-of hour of two in the afternoon. For a hungry young mountain lion, humans and deer pose similar problems in hunting: same size, same weight, same tendency to bolt when confronted. But deer run faster. On local-news shows in Southern California, footage of animal incursions is even more popular than film of freeway pileups. Lions and bears get the best Q-ratings: the mountain lion caught on home video as it races through the gated community of Woodland Hills; the sedated lion carried away by an impassive SWAT team; the black bear lolling in a backyard hot tub; the black bear digging its den under a condominium garage; the black bear hit by a car, limping dazed through a charmingly landscaped parking lot as shoppers stare.

My turf, *my* place, *my* real estate, *my* habitat, *my* home. Across the developed world, the daily competition for lebensraum among the wild, the cultivated, and the urban is as intense as the North American version. Roe deer, otter, mink, raven, cranes, and heron all but vanished from the urban scene soon after the Industrial Revolution, but in a postindustrial age are again being spotted in or near towns and cities both in Britain and on the Continent. In Bristol, urban wildlife managers report that red fox gather in urban gardens, watching television through open windows. Manchester Airport, second largest in the United Kingdom, has hired a full-time naturalist to protect flora and fauna as the airfield expands. So far, crews have moved sixteen thousand frogs and toads to new homes nearby, attracted four varieties of bat, diverted a river to preserve trout habitat, and created public housing for badgers whose original sett was overrun by construction. (The notoriously fussy and private badgers responded by breeding with enthusiasm in their elegant new den.) For the first time in centuries, wolves are harassing shepherds in Norway, in Spain's Asturian mountains, and in northern Italy. The famous urban ravens of Zurich are back, and Swiss motorists are discovering that the weasel-like Alpine stone marten adores gnawing through coolant hoses and ignition cables; Audi's head office estimates that ten thousand customers a year endure significant car chewing. In downtown Swinoujście, on the Polish-German border, a herd of wild boar, pushed out of their forest homes by development, have begun to bite tourists, invade public parks, and block traffic at city hall.

In Asia, wildlife increasingly persists in small islands of habitat, permanently marooned. Remote no longer means pristine: forty percent of the Himalayan forests have been lost to loggers. When pandas and elephants compete with humans for the same diminishing habitat, the animals nearly always lose. As land clearance continues to make rice fields and housing estates, as the region's population exponentially grows, the region's erosion problems soar, and so does its air pollution index, which in Calcutta or Malaysia can hit eight hundred. (A reading of three hundred is considered hazardous, the equivalent of smoking eighty cigarettes a day.) But sometimes nature still wins, as in New Zealand, where seventy million brushtail possums, an introduced species, are devouring twenty thousand tons of crops and native plants a day, or in Nepal, where community forestry has brought back both leopards and bears. Sometimes it's a standoff, as at the Indian air base south of New Delhi where panther attacks recently kept troops in barracks while nervous wildlife officials knelt beside runways lined with MIGs, trying to drive away the big cats with drums and cymbals. Urban Asia still sees clashes between the worlds; some of Bangkok's worst traffic jams occur when elephants break away from handlers and face down buses or fall into open manholes. Intensified Australian development has driven out many of the endemic species that were backyard staples as late as the 1960s, though imports thrive: in the suburbs of Adelaide, backyard gardening is frequently interrupted by cane toads the size of dinner plates, or by four-foot brown snakes, aggressive and venomous, which also like to live inside refrigerators and washing machines. Channel-billed cuckoos (roughly the size of vultures, but noisier) are nesting again in downtown Sydney after six decades away, and at least one golf course near Melbourne has so many kangaroos on the premises, eating the grass or following the sprinklers for water, that the resident pro has declared them in play: if you hit a 'roo, wherever the ball goes, the golfer goes too.

And in Japan, a crested ibis has hatched, to national rejoicing. The pale-peach ibis, which once flew over Tokyo by the thousands, is the ancient symbol of Japan, and evening's "ibis-colored sky" is a staple image in classical poetry. But by 1980, after decades of failed breeding attempts, the ibis was one specimen bird away from extinction in Japan, due to overhunting, pollution, and development. In 1999, the president of China gave the emperor of Japan two adult ibis. Months later, their chick, Yu-yu, was born, the first of its kind ever hatched in captivity, and an instant media celebrity.

Being a developer is the only influential American calling—except for journalism—that requires no license, and it shows: 80 percent of everything in America has been built in the last fifty years. During the 1990s, development of farmland and forest doubled, to a rate of 3.2 million acres a year. Some older industrial cities, like Chicago and Pittsburgh (and New York), try to encourage rehabbing and infilling, but their newer suburbs and exurbs, their galactic spume of housing developments and office parks and malls, are nearly always modeled on low-density, car-mad Sunbelt towns like Atlanta, where fifty acres of forest are felled each day to make suburbs for the 95,000 newcomers who arrive each year; like Las Vegas, which cheerfully admits it will run out of water by 2020; like Phoenix, where raging development devours Sonoran desert at the rate of an acre an hour.

Of all American cities, Greater New York is closest to build-out. In midtown Manhattan, values are calculated in thousands of dollars per square foot, and the extraordinary real estate prices within ninety minutes of the city are redefining "Manhattan commuter community" to include southern Vermont, the

Amish country of Pennsylvania's Lancaster County, and even Cape May, New Jersey, so far south that it lies below the Mason-Dixon line. Small and medium-sized cities struggle too. Madison, Wisconsin, had about 60,000 residents in 1960, and may soon reach 500,000; Tucson had 50,000 residents in 1940, and expects 1.2 million by 2025. The Interior Department confirms that scores of United States ecosystems have been destroyed, converted to agricultural use, or significantly degraded in the last fifty years, and the most imperiled areas are nearly all in the Northeast and the Midwest, California, the Rockies, and the Sunbelt; the correlation with the hot spots of American development is exact.

Terraforming, developers call it: defining the highest and best use of the land as a housing development, then bringing in the earthmovers to make the crooked straight and the rough places plain. Terraforming the United States from wild to working land has required, over six centuries, the destruction of 98 percent of America's original tallgrass prairie, 90 percent of its virgin forests, 80 percent of its pollution-filtering wetlands, and 80 percent of its wildlife. Now those hard-won farms and ranches are themselves endangered species. In a suburban nation, farmland takeover is much the fastest way to grow a cash crop of starter homes (defined in the New York region as four thousand square feet on a half-acre, minimum). The nine farm regions most threatened by development include California's Central Valley, where Los Angeles sprawl has finally broken through the mountains to consume the nation's richest agricultural land; the handsome swath of piedmont from south-central Pennsylvania through Maryland and upper Virginia; the secret valleys of the Driftless Region in southern Wisconsin and northwestern Illinois; the Texas Blackland Prairie around Dallas–Fort Worth; the Willamette and Puget Sound valleys; the whole southern tip of Florida; eastern Ohio's Till Plain; the lower Rio Grande Valley; and the New England–New York upland. The greenacres preservation programs of the northeast states are generous, but developers offer far more, especially in Connecticut's Litchfield Hills, Massachusetts's Berkshires, the high-tech exurbs of southern New Hampshire, the New Jersey horse country, and the Hudson River Valley. Onward, upward, outward: we are a service industry, developers say demurely, just responding to a community need.

They're right: by and large, Americans *like* the low-density life, crave the privacy of the air-conditioned house and heavily watered yard, insist on keeping the car keys, and enjoy the galactic city's scatteration of uses. As geese and deer accept the golf course as habitat and the sport-utility vehicle as predator, so fewer and fewer of us remember a common landscape in four sharp clear flavors: urban, suburban, cultivated, wild. The edge of town is becoming an idea from the postwar past, like dialing a phone, or putting on a record; suburban cul-de-sacs once rimmed by cornfield or woods now border only on other cul-de-sacs. Our only constant is the car culture. Autos outnumber people two-to-one in the United States, and 80 percent of that car use is one person per vehicle. Of *that*, 80 percent is personal errand-running, not the work commute, for a public that cares intensely about clean air and water but hardly at all about the big invisibles: ozone depletion, global warming, extinctions, the long-term costs of car addiction. The exception is Greater New York, much the furthest along the development continuum. Two in three New York–area residents say that their number-one worry used to be crime but is now the over-crowded life, defined and deformed by traffic and sprawl.

When natural encounters exceed what scientists politely call the cultural carrying capacity—the moment humans stop saying "Aww" and start calling 911—the true conflicts begin, and the true dilemmas. Never in American history have so many people lived near so many wild animals; never have our responsibilities as top predator, ethical and practical, been more unclear. For all our renewed encounters with next-door wildness, we know remarkably little about the new neighbors. We still don't understand how songbirds find their way from Patagonia to Scarsdale, or why tent caterpillars invade a particular urban forest, or how it is that grizzlies in Wyoming have begun to head *toward* the sound of a rifle, apparently aware they're likely to find a freshly killed animal, and an easily intimidated human. Maryland black bear are raiding farms again, eating sheep and plundering beehives. California foxes persist in killing rare native bird species. Florida bobcats kill endangered whooping cranes. Panicked deer jump through car sunroofs nearly everywhere. Even in Washington, D.C., deer have shown up just blocks from the White House. Washington now has more deer than lawyers.

There are twice as many coyotes in the United States today as in 1850; curious, well fed, and bored, they have taken to investigating parking garages and strip malls. (The coyote removed from an elevator in a Seattle federal building was described by the animal-control officer as "basically healthy, but a little stressed.") Three years after beaver traps were banned in Massachusetts, the state beaver population jumped from 18,000 to 55,000—more beaver than when the Pilgrims arrived—and the number of blocked waterways jumped too. Beavers weigh fifty pounds and can chew through a six-inch tree in fifteen minutes. They can turn streams into lakes and wasteland into meadow. When they apply their skills to a suburban landscape, they can block culverts, pollute wells, and flood parking lots. The state wildlife division would like to reinstitute a beaver harvest. Outraged environmentalists have countered with a beaver-vasectomy plan.

Even on New York's Upper East Side, wild creatures act—well, wild. On multimillion-dollar apartment terraces with Central Park views, the local red-tailed hawks (messy eaters all) will blithely rip up fresh-caught rats a foot from the Scalamandré curtains. In private rooftop gardens along Park Avenue, mallards arrive to nest in the imported planters, quacking, scatting, and resisting eviction attempts. On Staten Island, the forty-pound black swans of the botanic garden, fed up with visitors who poke them with sticks or smash new-laid eggs, have begun chasing tourists and staffers around their pond, biting as many of us as they can catch.

"I think I could turn and live with animals, they are so placid and self-contained," wrote Walt Whitman, the former editor of the *Brooklyn Eagle*. "I stand and look at them long and long." Princeton, New Jersey, where I live, is only an hour from New York, but its suburban drivers and gardeners struggle daily with deer and turkey who are less and less self-contained. Some of the best minds in American science are thwarted nightly here; string-theory physicists hang old CDs from tree branches to frighten off deer, professors of acoustical engineering concoct wondrous noise machines to keep township turkeys out of their azaleas. No luck. The Princeton deer take the sidewalk from garden to garden. The turkeys make garbage trucks and UPS vans wait while they cross the town's staid Colonial streets; on January nights, you can hear their metallic mating cries up on the hill behind the dry cleaner's and the video store.

Benjamin Franklin wanted the wild turkey as our national bird (instead of the cowardly and neurasthenic eagle) because it is hard to intimidate, adaptable, sociable, wily, and naturally patriotic: a cowl of scarlet wattle frames a small fierce head already ridged in white and blue. Wild turkey thrive today as an edge species, feeding along highway medians and parading through backyards from Atlanta to Milwaukee, yet just thirty years ago they were extremely rare, shot out in the East and hard to find in other regions. Around 1900, nearly as extinct as the buffalo, the remnant turkey flocks took refuge in the most isolated places they could find, from the Pennsylvania mountains to the Alabama swamps. But postwar restoration programs have been so successful that some four million birds now thrive nationwide. Conservation biologists are beginning to think that in the metropolis, any metropolis, there *is* no true wildlife anymore, only urban and suburban wildlife, adapting to yet another human-warped landscape with terrible patience.

I see turkeys nearly every day—commanding, demanding birds. Each carapace of feathers on each wide back is glazed like a scarab in obsidian and chestnut, with a bloom of rust or opal or emerald or peacock blue on breast and wing. A male herding three or four females will swell and gobble if they ignore him, spreading his war-bonnet tail; in June, pale fuzzy chicks struggle through the long grass beside the adults, cheeping and chirring, trying to keep up. By winter, they too will stand three feet high and weigh thirty pounds each, not quite wildfowl, but far from tame. Mostly the Princeton turkeys ground-feed, stalking about like dinosaurs, heads darting, talons flexing. They can fly at fifty miles an hour. They look like feathered beach balls when they do. And should two dominant birds unexpectedly meet, both rise straight up, screaming, to beat at one another in midair with their strong bronze wings, phoenixes beside a suburban birdfeeder.

In the last autumn of the last century, an unknown virus killed seven New Yorkers, sickened sixty-two, and infected nearly three thousand. At first, officials thought it might be an act of bioterrorism; ever since the bombing of the World Trade Center, city agencies have been haunted by the prospect of the suitcase nuke in the tunnel, the sarin release in the subway, the bucket of bacillus quietly emptied into New York's unguarded water reservoirs. The FBI was called in to investigate the deaths. And then the CIA. But as medical researchers struggled to find a pattern, and a name (was it malaria? bacterial meningitis? St. Louis encephalitis?), animal pathologists at the Bronx Zoo and the state lab began investigating a mystery of their own—the thousands of dead crows suddenly reported in and around New York. When members of the two investigations, criminal and natural, compared lab notes and blood samples, they realized that every metropolitan resident affected, crow or human, had been attacked by a single pathogen, the West Nile virus.

For public-health specialists, finding West Nile in New York was like turning the corner at Fifth Avenue and Central Park South and discovering the Great Pyramid of Giza where the Plaza Hotel should be. West Nile had been tracked in Asia, the Middle East, and central Europe, but never in the Americas. The virus is carried by migrating birds, like the robins and hawks I watched at the World Trade Center. Birds transmit the deadly virus to mosquitoes, which pass it to humans—an infectious cascade. A hundred thousand international flights arrive yearly at the New York airports; perhaps a mosquito bit a human who had contracted the disease overseas, or perhaps an infected bird was smuggled here in an air passenger's luggage or in the hold of an oceangoing vessel. It hardly matters, not in the age of the global food web and the cheap flight, when any germ on any continent can be twenty-four hours from Times Square.

For humans in the five boroughs, the odds of contracting West Nile are roughly a million to one; as a distinctly New York peril, it falls somewhere between death by rat bite and death by taxicab. The flu kills far more New Yorkers every year. But although the city tried spraying every borough with pesticide, tried persuading citizens (in eleven languages) to scrub out gutters and birdbaths, tried introducing larvae-eating mosquito fish to waste-treatment plants, New York remains a festival landscape for the common house mosquito that carries West Nile, a paradise of sewers, half-dried storm drains, and old tires left out in the rain. *Culex* breeds in stagnant water and loves city life. Unlike its rural cousin *Aedes*, which hunts mostly at dusk and dawn, *Culex* can feed all night, hibernate in the subways if the winter is mild, and will gladly fly ten miles for a blood meal; the carbon dioxide humans exhale stimulates it like champagne. Gotham held hostage by bugs delighted the world's media nearly as much as it disturbed the world's disease specialists.

Unleashed

When a jet-age virus unfriendly to humans colonizes a new hemisphere, the news is never good, even in a nation where the average citizen spends only seventy-two minutes outdoors each day, even in a city that often prefers its nature safely in museum dioramas, or else on a plate.

That fall I asked my students at New York University how they liked being prey. The graduate candidates in journalism tried to be even-handed and judicious, as their new profession demanded. They'd had a sobering week of mandatory police ride-alongs, replete with bar brawls, pit-bull fights, psychotic stalkers, and preadolescent holdup men. One contingent had even seen a body pulled from the Hudson near the Williamsburg Bridge, which their police escorts found mildly interesting, since late April to mid-May is the city's traditional floater season. (Spring and fall are the most active seasons for sky and water in Greater New York, as air masses race along the coast and lakes and rivers begin to turn over. Warming waters hasten decomposition, which produces internal gases, which make bodies buoyant.) But this was North America's warmest decade in a thousand years, and the New York rivers were giving up their numerous dead.

- Global warming is good for business, our policeman told us.
- All I know is, if I'm not out in nature once a week, I get sick.
- Nothing is more boring than nature. It's so motionless, like going to the opera.
- My mother called from Paris to say "Buy insect repellent. And remember that in cities, the only wildness is human."

- I'm a girl from Bed-Stuy. Nature is incidental. If I see a bird, okay, if not, not.
- I like walking in the woods and all that. But I would never go off the path.

The undergraduates were far more hostile, even for residents of a region that traditionally shows interest by criticizing. We had just read a passage by the social reformer Jacob Riis, in which he describes a New York slum child of the 1890s, taken to the country for a fresh-air vacation, who begs to go home because greenery hurts her eyes. The undergrads were instantly sympathetic. They had chosen a Greenwich Village campus, they said, to become film directors, documentarians, cultural critics, code poets. Not Ranger Rick.

- I'm the final product of natural selection, a fully urban creature.
- Natural to me means the Yankees should play on turf.
- You want urban wildlife, try *King Kong*, or maybe sale day at the Kate Spade store.
- Birds aren't cute. They're dangerous, rancid beasts.
- My boyfriend got sprayed in TriBeCa. It was three in the morning, he was very drunk, and the fogging-truck guys yelled at him to take cover but he didn't. He keeps renting *The Fly* and looking worried.

Would you rather spend the night in Central Park or at Astor Place and Broadway? I inquired.

Fifteen of sixteen voted for Astor and Broadway, despite the feral preteen huffers who congregate there. The dissenter, a westerner, argued that mountain lions have begun to eat joggers well within the Denver city limits, "which makes Central Park look like the Hyatt." Her course mates were adamant.

- Parks smell.
- Birds will poop on my head.
- Union Square is full of attack squirrels. They chase me.
- No people around means danger.
- Knowing seasons in New York does get hard. It's all stony and gray here. Mostly the displays in the store windows tell you.
- Nature is for summertime.
- I like weather. I go to Prospect Park to see weather.
- I'm a vegan, and I say don't kill the mosquitoes *or* the birds. They have a job to do too, you know.
- But birds shouldn't be allowed in the city if they endanger us.
- We'll get a great big net, see, and spread it between the Twin Towers, see . . .

The best student in the class, born in New Delhi but raised in Queens, said suddenly, "I went with my family to visit cousins in Perth Amboy once. I'd never been in the country before."

"You think Perth Amboy is the country?" said a Staten Islander.

"To me it is," said the Queens girl, simply. "There was a rabbit in their yard. I'd never seen a wild animal so close. I was *terrified*."

"How old were you?"

"Nineteen."

Our discussion was cut short by a hurricane. At the autumnal equinox, midway through the world's worst hurricane season in two centuries, New York City was meeting its first hurricane in decades, or the edge of one; the storm track ran from the commuting suburbs of north-central New Jersey across Long Island and out to sea. But the mayor began sending city workers home by noon, and businesses and campuses followed. Go home or be stranded, said the security guard who closed down our classroom at eleven-thirty. They say the subways might shut down at one P.M., maybe the bridges too. Go. Wrapped in slickers and ponchos and plastic trash bags, the undergraduates vanished into the noonday dimness, surefooting it across Greene Street's slick cobblestones, splashing down Waverly Place. I went the other way, through a rainswept, deserted Washington Square Park, clutching the Metro section of *The New York Times* over my head. Gray squirrels peered down at me from dry, warm tree holes.

I waded across Fifth Avenue and went to visit Manhattan's lost river. In the apartment-house lobby of 2 Fifth, beside the concierge desk, is a waist-high stone plinth, topped by a transparent cylinder full of water. "A brook winds its erratic way beneath this site," says the plaque nearby. "The Indians called it Manette, or Devil's Water. To the Dutch settlers it was Bestevaer's Killetje, or Grandfather's Creek, for two centuries familiar to this neighborhood as Minetta Brook."

The lobby fountain taps the underground flow, and today the Minetta was pulsing in its Plexiglas prison, clear and strong. Usually the Minetta is tea-colored. More often than not, it is invisible, especially when the building is having boiler trouble and the super shuts off the river entirely. "It likes storms," said the uniformed doorman. He takes a friendly interest in the secret stream, and knows its moods and freaks.

When New York was still New Amsterdam, colony maps showed brooks and springs and salt marshes all over Manhattan. The lively Saw Kill—*kill* is Dutch for "river" or "brook"— ran from what is now Park Avenue into the East River near present-day 76th Street. Montagne's Brook, wide enough for an island and two stout bridges, coursed from Eighth Avenue across Harlem to 107th Street. The seventeenth-century Minetta was a famous fishing stream, but by 1800 the city needed public spaces more than trout, and drained the Minetta marshes to make an execution site for criminals and a graveyard for yellow-fever victims; perhaps twenty-two thousand bodies remain in Washington Square Park today, beneath the dog runs and the chess tables. When New York's first building boom reached Greenwich Village in the 1820s, the reclaimed land became a military parade ground, though heavy guns sometimes caved in the drill-field surface, exposing the shrouded bodies of the dead. By the 1830s, the last Minetta farmers were selling out to developers, who put up handsome row houses to shelter downtown executives moving to the green and pleasant suburb of Greenwich Village. By the 1880s Minetta Water was paved over entirely to create Fifth Avenue; in the 1960s, Washington Square was closed to through traffic and made a rare downtown park, now (inch for inch) the most crowded recreational space in the world.

Beneath the underground chaos of cholera graves, hand-carved wooden waterpipes, and fiber-optic cable, Minetta Water still runs. New York is a river town embarrassingly short of real rivers, at least the one-way, freshwater sort. The neglected Bronx River is the city's sole wild watercourse, though its southern reaches are tidal, its fish toxic, and its bottom a midden of industrial archaeology: local volunteers detrashing one small stretch have hauled ashore rusted water heaters and mufflers, car tires and car motors, coils of barbed wire and curls of old lawn hose, bike wheels and bicycles, toasters and microwaves, oil cans and paint cans, TV antennas and TV sets, cable reels, fenceposts, Styrofoam packing, broken plate glass, shag carpets, broken toilets, plastic film, plastic milk boxes, old sweaters, used condoms, hypodermic needles, dead animal parts, fifty-five-gallon drums of unknown glop, kitchen sinks, and, once, an entire wine press.

The East River, which separates Manhattan from Queens, is not a river at all but a strait of saltwater and sewage-plant outflow connecting Long Island Sound and New York Harbor. The Harlem River is a tidal inlet. The Hudson is the Northern Hemisphere's southernmost fjord, and one of the world's great working rivers, but it is also estuarial. Twice a day, 260 billion cubic feet of seawater flow through the Narrows at high tide and race north, making the Hudson run backward for two hundred miles all the way to Troy; twice a day, nearly 80 million cubic feet of freshwater rush south to the Atlantic. But Minetta Water, sweet Minetta, still lives beneath Fifth Avenue and Greenwich Village. Almost every spring it rises, flooding the brownstone cellars along Downing Street or soaking the basement of New York University's law school. (In 1951, when the law quadrangle was being built, no one remembered the Minetta, except as the dimmest of urban myths. But the school's construction pit was a deep one; too deep. The Minetta, loosed once more, filled the site with fifteen thousand gallons of water a day.)

I walked west through the warm sheeting rain to Seventh Avenue, Minetta Water leaping beneath me in its dark channel all the way, and at Penn Station was swept down the narrow stairs to the westbound platform as a thousand Jersey commuters competed for space on the last train out of New York on a hurricane afternoon. It looked like the evacuation of Paris in 1940; people fought their way onboard carrying duct-taped trunks, birdcages, golf bags, photo albums, extra-large pizzas. At first, the train cars hummed with a cell-phone babble of cancellations and reschedulings, but as we began crossing the Meadowlands, even this hardened crowd fell quiet, watching the miles of emerald cordgrass and dark tidal inlet that separate city from continent. The aged iron bridges between New York and the mainland looked suddenly very fragile, the familiar industrial rivers strange and vast. As the train fled inland, we could see culverts and storm drains exploding like water cannons; abandoned cars sitting door-handle-deep; and soaked strangers in business suits forming impromptu rescue chains beneath a sky the blue-black of a new bruise. Floodwater swallowed the tracks, receded a touch under the harrying wind, then rose again. At the Newark station, a crowd of soaked commuters rushed the train doors, but were held back by police. We left them on the platform, staring hopelessly back up the empty tracks toward the city sunk in cloud.

Two hours later the metropolitan watersheds rebelled. Manhattan's West Side Highway flooded; North Jersey towns like Bound Brook saw seven feet of water suddenly rise in the streets; and in the city's northern suburbs commuters drowned on the way home, trapped by torrents that used to be backyard brooks. Mudslides swallowed houses; roads collapsed. The phones and the power went out. The rivers retook the purification plants. For ten days a million suburban New York customers boiled all their water to avoid gastroenteritis and cholera, took no showers, did no laundry. When repair crews at last broke into one major utility substation, they found a school of fish swimming in the control room.

The city of islands has been lucky in its enemies, so far. No natural or cultural disaster has ever forced it into all-out rehab, not like the Chicago fire of 1871, or the 1900 Galveston hurricane, or the Johnstown flood, or Atlanta and Richmond versus Sherman and Grant, or Dresden versus the B-29. Though New York was torched by the British during the Revolution (and burned again during the draft riots of 1863), war has never compelled this metropolis to confront its natural underpinnings, unlike the center of World War II London, where residents sowed wildflowers on bomb sites, and plants and birds not seen in town for a century reappeared to colonize the rubble, from rosebay willow herb to the black redstart. New York has not worried much lately about four-footed predators, unlike Berlin, where in the bitter winter of 1946–47 packs of wolves came out of the surrounding woods to hunt in streets and cellars. Nor have its panic grass and feverfew, which crave the sunny openness of New York vacant lots, ever rioted in sudden cell-deep confusion, growing in spirals or quintupling in size, as did the panic grass and feverfew of urban Hiroshima in the first radioactive weeks of the atomic age.

The natural world can tell us much about the life and death of cities, if we are willing to ground-truth. Ecologists call life on

Unleashed

Earth a shimmering disequilibrium, in which millions of species scrabble for food and shelter and family within the film of breathable air and drinkable water that skims the planet's surface like Saran Wrap on an orange. Yet the human urge to alter the experiment, to mess with the survival equation, to cast nature as ordeal or as enemy, is unabated. Humans are the first species to become a geophysical force, able to double the globe's nitrogen levels by burning fossil fuel and using chemical fertilizers to feed our urban billions, able to alter 50 percent of the planet's land surface, or so a recent Stanford study concludes: wetlands filled, prairies remade as cornfields, estuaries and coral reefs degraded by overfishing and pollution, freshwater aquifers drained in a decade of fossil water that took an eon to accumulate.

The mark of a successful civilization, Freud observed, is its control of nature. The New York metropolitan area is the world's most radical example of an environment sharply remade for human convenience; after three hundred years and a billion dollars invested, it ought to be the tamest place in America, with Los Angeles, Chicago, Washington, D.C., San Francisco, Philadelphia, Boston, Detroit, Dallas, and Houston close behind. Instead, the renewed possibility of dodging bears on the way to Pizza Hut brings us new riddles, and old mysteries: *Why won't nature stay where we tell it to? How much can we push, before it pushes back? And why should we care?*

Until recently, biologists believed that wild species persist most successfully at the heart of their particular geographic range, while populations at the edges may get stranded and die out. Now researchers think human activity spreads like a contagion. We may assume we're practicing chicken-pox development—a mall here, a subdivision there—but over time the human presence moves like a wave front, destroying and disturbing as it goes. Researchers are beginning to wonder how the urbanizing urge has affected *us*; the galactic city, it turns out, is not very healthy for a species hardwired for the Pleistocene.

New York spawns highly local medical syndromes, from trader's rotator cuff (found among those who work on commodities exchanges) to the stop-and-go whiplash of taxi neck. The average life expectancy for males born in New York has begun to decline, a reversal attributed largely to the city's AIDS epidemic. The very success of urban life, replete with indoor plumbing, immunizations, and antibiotics, seems to bore the human immune system to the point where it starts attacking itself: New York, rich in respiratory triggers like cockroaches and diesel fumes, is the nation's asthma capital, and in the Bronx, rates of death from the disease are triple those in the United States as a whole. Half of the twenty-one thousand daily commuters on the Long Island Railroad who travel more than eighty minutes one way have been declared severely sleep-deprived (and thus severely stressed) by New York University medical-school researchers. High blood pressure likewise dogs car commuters from New Jersey, who may need to rise at four-thirty A.M. to be at a Manhattan desk by nine. (In New York commuter society, anything under two hours each way is considered a "good" commute.)

New York makes you deaf: more than 40 percent of its younger residents already have a significant hearing loss. New York bombards you with far too much input: a single weekday edition of *The New York Times* (information scientists gleefully point out) contains more fact than the average person absorbed in an entire lifetime in Shakespeare's England. New York is the epicenter of American stress: just being in the city raises one's chance of stroke or heart attack by 55 percent, especially among visitors not adapted to local conditions. That classic dispassionate observer, the anthropologist from Mars, would likely conclude that New York's best adjusted and most successful species are grasses and ants, motor vehicles and tall buildings, pigeons and rats. The number of trees within the city is falling all the time, and human numbers are merely holding steady; without the tonic of immigration, New York would lose population, most years. But cars and roaches and, most of all, rats daily expand their domain.

The city rat is what every epidemiologist fears: an omnipresent, intelligent carrier with a track record. Rat saliva, rat droppings, and rat fleas all carry disease, from typhus to plague to rat-bite fever. The city of New York has eight million people, but twenty-eight million Norway rats, maybe more—some rat gurus claim four for every human, others think a more accurate rat/human ratio is six or seven or even eight to one. When Rudolph Giuliani saw yet another monstrous specimen run squeaking across the porch at Gracie Mansion, he announced yet another all-out cleanup. Rat war is a New York mayoral tradition, but neither public nor private exterminators believe we can ever win, though several hundred city employees do nothing but pursue the city's rats, baiting trap after trap with sardines and peanut butter.

Like deer, like coyote, like raccoons, like falcons, rats adapt brilliantly to the New York infrastructure. In Brooklyn, rats have been observed jumping into subway cars, waiting politely under the seats, then getting off at the next stop. New York rats, also called brown rats or Norway rats, are not endemic to North America. To move from their native Asia to Europe, they stowed away on merchant ships and military transports; when the British sailed into New York Harbor in 1776 to blockade the city, brown rats waited in the cargo holds. Some of their descendants in the city's sewers are seventeen inches long. (When the Parks Department imported owls to kill New York rats the natural way, the owls, no fools, quickly switched to mice.) Rats love sewers. They can tread water for three hours, swim half a mile, squeeze through pipes the size of a quarter, and raise family after family in the warm redolent darkness, up to 150 rat pups per rat lifetime. Since a rat must eat one-tenth of its body weight each day, they scavenge our wastes with ferocious concentration. Rats like subway tunnels too; so much so that the Metropolitan Transit Authority must supplement its poisoning program with the Vak Trak, a French-made cleaning train that sucks up every bit of subway litter in its path: hypodermic needles, beer bottles, used tampons, antique pastrami sandwiches, and live rats, which explode.

Rats like to socialize, just not with us. Lords of the night city, with territorial maps as precise as any falcon's, they avoid humans whenever possible. In the country, rats may live in packs of up to two hundred, capable of killing piglets and lambs. In cities, they form smaller but even more aggressive gangs. One New York rat population traditionally summers in Central Park but invades East Side apartment buildings when the weather cools. Another tenacious pack defends the Manhattan end of the Brooklyn Bridge, terrorizing pedestrians. Morningside Heights, near Columbia, is a famous rat zone; park your car on the street overnight, and by morning the local rats may have built a nest in the engine. In a single warehouse near the Lincoln Tunnel, ten thousand rats were recently found.

Rat teeth, like beaver teeth, never stop growing. Fortunately, the underground city is full of satisfying material to gnaw: cables, wiring, insulation, aluminum, even concrete. New York rats regularly crash Internet servers and set off security systems. Rats are smart: although a fast-forward version of natural selection has made rats in many big cities immune to nearly all conventional poisons, they still may press one pack member into service as a taster; if the test rat dies, the others resolutely avoid the bait. (In lab studies, rats have even learned to tell Schubert from John Coltrane, pushing a lever to get food when classical music plays, abstaining during jazz selections.) Most of all, rats like to explore. All over New York, exterminators report, they will climb up sewer lines and emerge, soaked but triumphant, through apartment toilets—*sixteenth-floor* apartment toilets, in some cases—which is why, even in the fancier Manhattan zip codes, you may notice a big heavy brick on the toilet lid.

Ethologists—animal-behavior experts—are often drawn to Manhattan, Bedford Stuyvesant, and the South Bronx because these sections of New York offer such fine open-air labs for the study of mammals in an overcrowded space, a condition they call a sink. To the expert eye, New York is a people sink of thrilling proportions. Birds and mammals seem to need a certain amount of real estate to live in, and cannot tolerate overcrowding beyond a certain point. If too many try to inhabit a finite area, the classic result is a die-off, a population crash, sometimes from the toxic effects of excess adrenaline—produced by the body in response to the constant stress of living too close to too many other members of its own species—and sometimes from disease, a new virus or bacterial strain whose rough justice edits a population back to levels the environment can bear.

Human New York (scientists delicately note) is overdue for this sort of correction, which is one reason the stealthy arrival of the West Nile virus made so many so nervous, particularly in a time when environmental disruptions and international travel are returning us to preantibiotic conditions. Regional and national borders, notes the World Health Organization, are meaningless now, whether the problem is an airborne infection, like tuberculosis or influenza, or a disease passed through the drinking-water supply (like cryptosporidium, which killed four hundred people in Milwaukee in 1994), or one contracted by insect bite, like malaria or West Nile. In the new geopolitics of disease, far-traveling bacteria, viruses, and parasites evolve faster than we do, and brush off our best efforts at containment. In 2000, the United States declared AIDS a destabilizer of governments around the world, and thus a threat to national security. But the great nineteenth-century urban plagues are back in the developed world too, as global commuters. As military doctors visited the emergency rooms of Brooklyn and the Bronx during the crime-wave eighties to learn how to treat bullet wounds, so physicians and medical researchers in Paris, Milan, Los Angeles, Chicago, Denver, Miami, and New York must relearn the treatment of diphtheria, dengue fever, and yellow fever.

Some of the new drug-resistant strains can be passed by a handshake, by choosing the wrong seat at the movies, by using the phone in a neighboring office cubicle, by standing within range of a sneeze on the subway. In a sink like New York, pathogens are democratic and Darwinian. Their random targets—the Wall Street analyst, the West Side private-school teacher, the Silicon Alley executive—are good at denial. *"I floss, I kick-box, I pop down to Brazil, I buy my lamps in SoHo and my lunch at Balducci's. I can't have drug-resistant TB . . . malaria . . . the plague." That's* medieval. You go home to your small expensive apartment, stare at the brick on your toilet, and brood.

As an urban-survival strategy, it's been tried, with distressing results. Consider that classic pandemic and citykiller the Black Death, which seems to have originated in China or India but was carried overland to the Black Sea and to the port cities of Italy and southern France via the Mediterranean shipping fleets, the 747's of medieval commerce. Beginning in the spring of 1348, illness moved north along highways and trade routes until every European nation was affected except Poland, which set up a strict border quarantine, and Bohemia, protected by mountains. High fever, aching limbs, vomiting blood, and blackened, swollen lymph nodes in armpits and groin were hallmarks of the disease. Those who contracted it generally died in four terrible days, though Boccaccio tells us that in some cases the infection developed so swiftly that people "ate lunch with their friends and dinner with their ancestors, in Paradise."

The Black Death was really a series of intense local epidemics, each lasting four to six months, and worst in cities and towns. Responses to the emergency varied enormously. Fourteenth-century cities like Paris had fairly good public sanitation—certainly no worse than Victorian London—but this sort of international disaster was beyond the reach of any city council. People improvised, ringing bells and firing cannon to clear the air, breathing through kerchiefs drenched with sulphur and rosemary to keep away contagion. The medical establishment weighed in with a number of remedies, mostly conflicting: exercise and nap, don't exercise *or* nap, eat rich strengthening foods, stick to a low-fat diet, keep warm, take cold baths, think calm thoughts. Everyone tried to avoid crowds. In winter, the disease seemed to disappear, but only because the vector insects were dormant. In spring, the deaths resumed.

Contemporary science had no understanding of how the disease was passed along: bad air? polluted water? Citizens and officials tended to blame poison in the water supply, introduced by unknown enemies. The poor blamed the rich, the rich the poor. Lepers were a popular suspect, as was any outsider, any stranger. Nearly everyone blamed the Jews. The plague outbreaks in Europe were accompanied by the greatest mass killing of Jews in history before the twentieth century.

The Black Death was the worst catastrophe to strike western Europe in a thousand years, the most terrible event since the fall of Rome. It killed more people than World War I and World War II combined, and did so much, *much* faster. Europe's population in 1347 was 75 million; in 1352, 50 million. *Media vita in mortua sumus*, people whispered; in the midst of life, we are in death. In Pisa, 80,000 died in eight months. At Oxford, university enrollment fell from 30,000 to 6,000 between one year and the next, as students and faculty succumbed to disease, or set out for home across a continent in chaos. Europe had come close to social and economic disaster during the great famine of 1315–22, when climate shifts abruptly ended a century of benign weather, and unusually bitter winters and rainy summers destroyed seven harvests in a row and brought on urban bread riots and cult manias of equal violence. Malnutrition begat class warfare; environmental history shaped social history with unusual speed. But the plague years were infinitely worse. In twenty months, one out of every three people in Europe was dead. Over the next century, counting later sporadic outbreaks, historians believe the total population of Europe fell by two-thirds.

Educated urban professionals were especially hard-hit—physicians, clergy, academics. Many stayed in their dying cities to help the suffering as best they could, and died themselves. Historians died in mid-chronicle; writers in mid-poem; the king of Spain and the queen of France, in mid-reign. Pandemic, famine, and civil disruption marked the Black Death's second year. The sick became the enemy, and Death a terrorist, no longer the gentle Sister Death, praised by Saint Francis of Assisi, who safeguarded the soul in the hope of resurrection. To ask neighbors or officials for help meant the starkest of human choices, since urban-quarantine authorities could immediately force all members of an infected household into a municipal pesthouse. Entering a plague hospital was almost always a death sentence, even for the healthy. Neighbor informed on neighbor; city couples abandoned their children or their elderly and fled to the country—managing only to spread contagion farther and faster. Lawyers refused to come out of their houses to make wills for the dying. Funerals stopped, because priests and gravediggers were often among the dead; stacks of bodies rotted in churchyards until they could be buried in mass pits or thrown into an urban river hastily consecrated for the purpose. Some people joined a new mass movement of flagellants, self-proclaimed martyrs who moved from town to devastated town, beating themselves with whips and flails to appease an unresponsive God. Others chose defiance, holding orgies and gambling parties atop new graves. Prostitutes solicited for trade in the cemeteries. Looting by the urban poor rose. The Hundred Years' War was called off, for lack of troops, but soon resumed.

Yet, if you take the long view, as historians tend to, this particular population die-off by *Homo sapiens* resulted in more intensive use of capital, more powerful technology, more diversified investment, and higher living standards for the poor: a world badly shaken, and noticeably improved. After three terrible years, Europe's peasants began agitating for better wages and more rights, and young people everywhere left the land to learn skilled trades in the recovering cities, creating rural depopulation but urban vigor, as the formerly closed guilds were forced to recruit. But Europe did not regain its preplague population levels for three hundred years.

What was the Black Death? Even now, no one is sure. Typhus has been suggested, or a high-mortality virus like the 1919 flu, which killed twenty million around the world, or anthrax, or even an early form of AIDS. Medical historians traditionally identify the Black Death as bubonic plague, since plague is carried by rats, which move well by ship, and are ceaselessly bitten by fleas, which then bite people, regurgitating into humans the infected rat blood. The rat dies, the people die, the flea lives on. If the Black Death was indeed bubonic plague, several strains may have been simultaneously at work—pneumonic, which

destroys the lungs, and septicemic, which attacks the blood.
More than two hundred Americans have died of bubonic
plague since the early 1990s. *Yersina pestis* has been active in
the western states for years, carried, like hantavirus, by squirrels, skunks, rats, and mice. Recently, new cases have been
recorded in New England, mid-Atlantic, and southeastern
states.

A medium-sized American city like Eugene, Sacramento,
Fort Wayne, or Raleigh-Durham might well be able to beat
back a rat-borne plague, though sometimes killing rats only en-
courages fleas to find human hosts. In contemporary New York,
a rat-borne plague of any kind would be extremely bad news.
The great port of Venice, before the Black Death struck, was
the New York of its time, and at least three-quarters of its population died within the epidemic's first year. For equivalent effect, think of a supervirus, deliberately or accidentally let loose,
that depopulates all of Manhattan, all of Brooklyn, and still
leaves three million refugees fighting to reach an equally
plague-stricken Newark, Stamford, or White Plains.

For the field biologist or the environmental historian, any
urban disease outbreak is also a Darwinian memo, a pointed re-
minder that the natural world remains the city's largest con-
stituency, from the rainforest of bacteria in your basic New York
mouth (five hundred varieties, at last count) to the millions
of air, land, and water creatures determined to make their
homes in the five boroughs and their metropolitan sprawl.
Some, like the horseshoe crab, were here to greet the
dinosaurs. Others, from turkeys to deer, are returning to their
historic territories. Some crossed an ocean to get here, such
as the brown rat, or the West Nile virus. All of them like the

New York life—the pathogens, the vectors, and the charismatics, especially.

One recent flawless June day, I went with two Princeton University naturalists to visit northern New Jersey's Walpack Valley, which lies in the low mountains near the Delaware Water Gap. Because it is so close to Interstate 80, New York–area commuters have begun to settle the area in earnest, but along the steep-sided Walpack the year could easily be 1740, or 1440. Driving a narrow road through the valley at sundown, all three of us watch the asphalt and not the scenery. But one of the naturalists has good peripheral vision.

"Bears! Back up."

Bears in the North Jersey rhododendron thickets? We look at each other with wild surmise. Four black bears are wandering a swampy glade not thirty yards away. One rubs meditatively against a stand of ashes along the water meadow edge, then stretches up at full height to incise on the silvery bark a message for ursine passersby: "Alert! Something very large lives here!" A sow works a patch of low blueberry bushes, drawing up the fruit-heavy branches with one massive paw and lipping each clean. "At least four hundred pounds," the senior naturalist whispers, impressed despite himself. The black bears of New Jersey are among North America's largest, as big as those in Yosemite, or Alaska. Sated, the female turns to nudge a balky yearling up the path. He wants to play in the pond; she wants him to learn where berries grow. He is the size of a large hog, and she is larger than two sumo wrestlers; she prevails. The last of the bears, turning from the water's edge, glances at us unmoved, quarters the clearing, then also stretches up, up, up along a birch trunk.

Ursus major, his mark. Three humans look at four bears. Only we are awed.

Boston has a law, passed in 1634 and still on the books, that requires anyone crossing Boston Common to carry a gun for defense against bears. The city of New York does not encourage such rural nostalgias. For a long time now, the only bears in town have been the bears of Wall Street; the Coney Island Arctic Ice Bears Club, whose members plunge into the Atlantic for the cameras each New Year's Day; and Gus the neurotic polar bear at the Central Park Zoo, the one with his own behavioral therapist. Yet black bear, I know, have been sighted in the Trenton suburbs, in industrial New Brunswick, and in the parking lot of Princeton's Institute for Advanced Study; they are my local fauna now. In the early 1970s, New Jersey had almost no bears left. Now it has more than a thousand, and residents are complaining about the bear crime rate, even as development pushes a new tier of commuter suburbs into prime bear territory. The most crowded state in the Union remains 40 percent forest and 20 percent wetland; it's good bear country. But so many bears have broken into suburban houses, or wandered into heavy traffic, or advanced, whuffling with curiosity, toward groups of awed schoolchildren, that New Jersey may reinstate its bear season, in a region that hasn't needed a serious bear hunt since King George III held the property deeds.

"How far are we from Manhattan right now?" I ask the senior naturalist as we wait for the bears to move on. He lowers his field glasses and points straight east, through the beech trees and spicebush.

"Forty miles, maybe less. There's a fire tower at the top of this hill. Climb it, and with a good pair of field glasses you can see the World Trade Center, easy."

In the exurban summer twilight, the bears turn to gaze at us once more, two tons of confident predator, entirely unruffled, entirely unhuman. They walk away in single file, wet sable muzzles lifted to scent the night wind. They are heading straight toward Times Square.

Two

Leaf and Stone

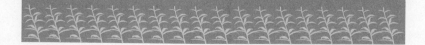

The Shores of Brooklyn

The placid neighborhoods near Sheepshead Bay, where south Brooklyn meets saltwater, entirely lack the industrial gloom of old port districts like Red Hook, majestic though in ruin. Urban rehabbers trek here, shrug, and return to desirable Park Slope. There are no historic brownstones to discover, no cobbled streets. This is backcountry, low-rise Brooklyn, once a summer beach resort; add some maples, and you could be in Sault Sainte Marie; put in cypress, and it could be Apalachicola. No-name marinas dot the shoreline, each with its seafood bar and grill. Retirees fish at pierside in aluminum deck chairs, coolers and bait buckets about their feet. Middle-schoolers in veteran rowboats explore ragged sandbars and willow-shaded coves, looking (not too hard) for presupper adventure. In the polluted creeks of the Brooklyn-Queens border, eel catchers ply their ancient trade. Manhattan's teakettle intensity is eight miles and a bridge, a tunnel, a world, away.

When Brooklyn was America's fourth-largest city, just after the Civil War, its commissioners hired Frederick Law Olmsted and Calvert Vaux to create a grand thoroughfare from Prospect Park to Coney Island. Central Park's designers delivered an avenue to rival the boulevards of Paris and Berlin. Ocean Parkway still bisects Brooklyn, lined with close-set brick apartment buildings, each with its strictly clipped rectangle of lawn. In the early-June dusk, a gilded new moon rises above its double lanes of slow traffic, Brooklyn's urban paseo. The heat index today was 107 degrees, and even at half past eight the evening air is tropical, yet all along the avenue young men stand at curbside in neat dark suits and hats; many wear the distinctive side curls of the Hasidim, the most orthodox of Jewish sects. Holding their children's hands, they watch the violet sky, waiting to count the first three stars, and mark the Sabbath's start. As on every New York Friday, public-service announcements on city radio stations have broadcast the precise moment of sunset ("Candlelighting . . . is at . . . eight . . . thirty-six . . . exactly"), and in a thousand parkway windows, women with aprons over their good clothes dart about, adding last swift touches to Sabbath dinner tables.

Roads in this part of Brooklyn tend to end suddenly, in thickets of beach grass and tall tough phragmites, as happens if you follow Ocean almost to the sea, then turn for Gerritsen Avenue and the lower edge of Marine Park, where a quarter-mile of sand dune separates salt-lagoon marsh from beach mudflat. Here fireflies have begun to rise and wander, bright as the headlights on the Belt Parkway just ahead. Pleasure craft moving down the channel sound their boat horns as they pass. A gambling cruise trails the amplified beat of a live band. A pair of lean mackerel tabbies, feral cats of the marsh, burst from cover and dash past the B31 bus. New York's green-space holdings, though large, are not evenly spread, and no other New York borough has a worse ratio of parkland to people. Brooklyn has 2.3 million human inhabitants, but only 1.7 acres of public green space for every thousand residents. Even Manhattan has 1.8 acres. (Boston, the next worst case, supports 4 acres of park per thousand residents. Most American cities offer at least 6, except for Los Angeles, where the ratio is one-tenth of a public green-space acre per citizen.)

Beside the meager dune path wait half a dozen urban rangers from the Parks Department, businesslike men and women in their twenties wearing snappy Smokey the Bear hats and carrying radios and handcuffs, but no guns. Should we encounter illegal dumpers, they will make arrests and call for backup. Parks work in New York is a constant struggle to discourage citizens from rolling pesticide drums into city rivers or shoving flaming cars off the overpasses into city forest. Three dozen doughty nature fans, aged twelve to eighty, follow the rangers single file into the tangle of beach grass as jets whine overhead, heading across Jamaica Bay to the runways of JFK. But in the sheltering arm of the cove, where landscape becomes seascape, the Brooklyn shore is dark, and private, and restless with horseshoe crabs. New York's original commuters, harmless, mysterious, horseshoe crabs live thirty years as individuals, and eons as a species. For 360 million years, they have come to lower Brooklyn to mate and lay their eggs. Their nearest neighbors, the borough's hundred thousand Hasidim, are living fossils too, keeping the eighteenth century a daily and living presence in cyber-age Flatbush. But the horseshoe crabs were here when Brooklyn and Europe were next-door land masses; here when the moon hung low and huge in the Devonian sky; here to salute the dinosaurs that once roamed New Jersey and Queens.

Most of the year, horseshoe crabs cruise the sandy coastal waters off New York, Delaware Bay, and the Yucatan, quietly hunting sea worms and mollusks. Horseshoe crabs are primitive arthropods, distantly related to spiders and scorpions. Their blood is bright blue, their mating habits precise. In May and June, as water temperatures rise past 70 degrees, crab pheromones intensify. In groups that can range between five and twenty, the crabs begin to form sex chains, paddling langorously a few inches off Brooklyn until the females decide to come ashore, carrying or towing the smaller males. A ponytailed ranger points out a female crab half-buried in sand, digging hard, preparing an oval depression for the twenty thousand pale green eggs she will lay tonight, each one the size of a sesame seed. To fertilize them, she will seize a male crab and drag him across the secret nest. The ranger reaches into the sea and holds up a second, struggling female, as big as a dishpan, with a hard curved shell the shape and color of a rusted iron horseshoe, and a rigid tail like a stingray's lash. Horseshoe crab design has changed very little in two hundred million years; as the flashlight beam plays over her belly, we inspect the twelve eyes and five pairs of walking legs, the tiny food-grinding mouth spines, and the flinching translucent book gills, delicate as tissue paper, that let her leave the water just long enough to deposit her eggs before she is swept out to the continental shelf, and the great deeps. Horseshoes only look ferocious. They have no teeth and no claws; the pincers gently squeeze; the long tail steers, not stings. As mad, unbridled crab sex goes, the Brooklyn edition at our feet is sedate, even stately. The Delaware Bay version (rangers explain wistfully) is much jazzier, with writhing heaps of mating crabs, and hundreds of thousands of birds swooping in to feast on surplus eggs.

The big female is carefully returned to the water, and leaves in a hurry—dinosaurs were never *this* much trouble—to continue socializing in the intertidal zone. The sea edge is the place where most higher animals evolved, but it is also one of Earth's harshest environments, since its inhabitants are continually covered and exposed, especially on a night like this, when sun, moon, and Earth are lined up, keeping the gravitational pull strong and the tides high to create an upwelling, or spring, tide. (At the half-moon, sun and moon will be at right angles, pulling against each other; the tides become less marked, and are known as neap, or scarce, tides.) Since we swing closest to the sun in June and December, high and low tides in these months are most extreme, and best for crab-carrying. The world's only other ocean crabs are found off India, Indonesia, and Japan. All are endangered, thanks to the loss of their Asian breeding grounds to shoreline development, plus relentless overfishing. The horseshoe crabs of the eastern seaboard are in trouble too: since 1992, their numbers have declined by 50 percent, a population crash so swift that the Atlantic states now limit the crab harvest. Five million pounds of crab are taken in United States waters every year. Commercial fishermen consider them good bait for eel and conch. Agribusiness dices them into fertilizer. The medical industry covets horseshoe crabs as natural detectors of bacterial toxins in surgical implants, prosthetics, pacemakers, and medications; federal law requires that intravenous drugs be tested with horseshoe crab blood. So drug companies and biomedical device–makers spend fifty million dollars a year to capture horseshoe crabs, bleed them, and extract a toxin-sensitive substance called limulus amoebocyte lysate; the crabs that survive the procedure are released back into the ocean.

A major hemispheric bird migration depends on horseshoe crabs too. A million shorebirds time their spring flights from South America to include a crucial feeding stop at the mid-Atlantic beaches just as the crabs make their annual trek ashore. The piping plovers are heading for the Arctic; the ten-ounce red knots have come ten thousand miles from Tierra del Fuego and have twenty-five hundred nonstop miles yet to fly. The only way either bird can survive the last push northward is to double its weight by gorging on new-laid crab eggs. The pandemonium on the beaches from Virginia to New York—the survival dance of millions of birds and thousands of crabs under a June moon—is the keystone of a one-hundred-million-dollars-a-year wildlife-watching industry. But strip-mining the crabs has brought the bird counts down, way down. Another set of population crashes in the night.

Yet above the Brooklyn shore, this night's new moon has turned from gold to silver, and crab fanciers are spread out along the sands, flashlights on low, following but not frightening the trios and knots and locomotive chains of horseshoe crabs that dig and drag and clasp and swim. I come upon an ardent pair moving through the shallows, the male pushing the female along like a tug guiding a liner. Slowly, he charts and evades the flotsam of the wrack tide, the floating Snapple bottle, the bent malt-liquor can, the waterlogged copy of *ESPN Sports*, the tattered barbeque-chicken bag. The Snapple bottle, as smooth and empty as a shell, interests him briefly. Build thee more stately mansions, O my soul. But intent on prehistoric duty, he swims on. I watch until three stars rise from the runways across the water, and then three more, while the ebb tide carries them both into Sheepshead Bay, toward the unresting sea.

Horseshoe crabs are definitely native New Yorkers. Woolly mammoths would be, if prehistoric global warming had not sent them north and west. And for some human New Yorkers, the city truly is home: time spent anywhere else seems camping, or exile. But for other New York residents, human and wild, the megacity remains a fancier version of the Dutch trading post it used to be: North America's chief port of entry, a processing station for goods and information, a greased chute into a new life in a new world. New York may be a riveting experiment in extreme democracy and extreme capitalism—so, how rich *can* we get, if we don't all kill each other first?—but the rigors of the cultural crucible, not to mention the shopping, have always crowded out much discussion of what it means to become native to a place, at least in the way geographers and environmental historians mean it:

Can you point north?
Describe where your garbage goes?
Name three trees you pass on the way to work?

Responsibility born of understanding can be a tough sell here, when the topic is watersheds, or community gardens, or the ozone layer. In Maine or Arizona, the landscape is itself a lesson, but in topography as in history, New York erases as it goes.

Leaf and Stone

Let the mayor take care of it; that's what I pay taxes for.
Does New York even have an environment?
I loathe trees. People are what count.

Commuters, ancients, victims, entrepreneurs, pioneers, revenants. Immigrants. Invading aliens. Even the severest scientific observers resort to anthropomorphized language and evolutionary metaphor to describe arrivals and departures in the natural city—in hey-watch-your-mouth New York, a risky act. Post-1970 immigration has steadily remade the United States into two nations—the intensely diverse America of the coastal ports of entry (New York, San Francisco, San Diego, Houston, Boston, Washington, Miami, Chicago) and a new kind of white flight, discreet but definite, to Minneapolis, Denver, Orlando. Only 21 of the nation's 325 metropolitan areas are truly multicultural. More than three-fourths of this most recent immigrant wave went to just six states: California, Texas, Florida, Illinois, New Jersey, New York. A third of contemporary New Yorkers are "new" immigrants—Russians, eastern Europeans, Chinese, Koreans, East Indians, Arabs, Turks, Mexicans, Dominicans—and in their energetic presence, the older narratives of Irish, Italian, WASP, and Jewish New York are starting to sound quaint and dim, urban romances from that foreign country, the past. The city is much less Jewish than it used to be, demographers note: in 1950, 2.1 million Jews lived in the five boroughs; today only one million do, plus another half million in the metro suburbs. The young are intermarrying, or venturing to other regions, or both; the old seek the sun; the city's cultural mix churns on. Without its keystone ethnics, will New York be New York? No one knows. In the twenty-first-century city, 180 languages are spoken, to the school board's despair; the last time the city turned so polyglot was the ragtime decade of 1900–10, when it had 48 foreign-language newspapers (not to mention two daily mail deliveries).

The same turbulence and messy energy applies to non-human New York. Some local life-forms pretty clearly *are* immigrants, like the very colorful, very vocal Central American parrots, probably descended from escaped pets, that nest in a Bronx ballpark near Fordham University, enjoying the warmth of the arc lights. Other parrots have nested beneath aluminum house siding in Queens, and one rogue band tried to settle in Central Park. Winter birders in three boroughs have seen parrots playing happily in the snow. Monk parakeets from Argentina—raucous, bright green, and more than a foot tall— have built giant nests near Brooklyn College and in Brooklyn's Greenwood Cemetery, a spot that lives in birding infamy, since nature lovers made the big mistake in 1851 of releasing there a few European house sparrows—previously unknown in North America—which spread from coast to coast even faster than the fifty English starlings loosed in 1889 Manhattan by an eccentric manufacturing tycoon named Schiefflin, a Shakespeare fancier who believed all the bard's birds should be represented in North American skies ("I'll have a starling shall be taught to speak / Nothing but 'Mortimer.'" *Henry IV*, I). The linnets and nightingales died of culture shock, but the starlings founded a genetic empire: 300 million live in the United States today. Likewise, ring-necked pheasants, sent to friends in Oregon by an American consul general stationed in Shanghai, soon joined the escapee roster and now range from South Dakota to New Jersey, as house finches from the western United States escaped from a New York pet dealer in the 1940s to become bird-feeder regulars throughout the East.

When does an immigrant become an alien invader? When it starts to cost us money, usually. Releases of species not native to this continent, intentional and accidental, have greatly changed the nature of nature in America. Biologists estimate that four thousand plants and twenty-three hundred animals have arrived here from abroad, riding in cargo holds, in ballast water, in smugglers' underwear. The southern states worry most about fire ants, the lake-strangling water hyacinth, the eucalyptuslike melaleuca trees introduced to Florida in the 1930s, and kudzu. In the Great Lakes and Great Plains, the zebra mussel has been a worrying freshwater intruder, though not yet as invasive as crabgrass, or the viciously entangling multiflora rose, or purple loosestrife (brought to North America by 1860s European shipping), which chokes out reeds and reduces wetland habitat. In the Southwest, salt cedar, the Africanized honeybee, and the cotton boll weevil are at least as destructive as the commercial cactus rustlers who dig up saguaros by night, then sell them at caviar prices to developers and Xeriscapers. California and the intermountain West must contend with wild pigs and cheatgrass, the rosy wolfsnail, the Russian olive, and the Mediterranean fruit fly. Buckthorn, the green crab, and the common carp continue to afflict the American Northeast.

Some nonnative species are practically members of the DAR, like that eighteenth-century stowaway the Norway rat. Garlic mustard, which smothers native wildflowers like bloodroot and hepatica, escaped from specimen herb gardens of the 1860s; water chestnut, which, like hydrilla, forms a choking mat on rivers and ponds, was spotted in the United States by the

1880s. European gypsy moths escaped from their cages during an 1869 storm and started eating oaks; by the 1990s, the much more destructive Asian strain slipped into the United States aboard grain freighters arriving in the Pacific Northwest. As international trade accelerated in the early twentieth century, so did natural invasions. An extremely efficient Asian blight, first seen in New York City, spread through eastern woodlands, stripping 200 million acres of their strong and beautiful American chestnuts by the end of the 1920s. Dutch elm disease was introduced to the East Coast in 1931, thanks to a shipment of infected elm wood from France. Like New Haven, Connecticut, New York used to be a city of magnificent American elms. So far, the disease has killed 77 million trees, in dozens of states, and entemologists expect similar destruction by the Asian long-horned beetles, probably stowaways in Chinese-made packing crates, now destroying thousands of trees in Brooklyn, Manhattan, and Chicago. The tree that grew in Brooklyn, *ailanthus altissima*, the tree-of-heaven, is itself an Asian introduction.

Some scientists call these biological events smart pollution: biospecies posing new dangers in places they don't belong. They may outcompete the native plants and animals, or they may evolve with striking speed to match local conditions, preparing to dominate and even destroy. Chemical spills are dumb, biologists remind us; they cannot reproduce, they have a half-life, they will, eventually, dissipate. Bio-pollution spreads, stretches, and makes itself at home in a borderless biosphere in which Formosan termites turn the antebellum architecture of New Orleans's French Quarter to sawdust and Chinese mitten crabs invade the Sacramento–San Joaquin Delta, California's main water source. Every fourteen weeks, some new species establishes itself in the San Francisco area alone. Any nation with an airport, a dock, a car ferry, or a postal service needs to worry, since the traffic in displaced species works both ways; introduced Atlantic jellyfish are thriving in the Black Sea, tree snakes from New Guinea have overrun Guam, and South American water hyacinth chokes lakes in Africa and China. But botanists still love to study New York, because it is such a biological Noah's Ark—the city now has more exotic plants than native ones—and a perfect field station for watching the natural world redefine a city with guerrilla persistence, reaching and twining in the night, leaf by tendril by thorn.

Of all American environments, the New York area is the most forcibly simplified and disturbed. When humans cause ecological chaos, plants take advantage. Trillium and ginseng like a quiet life, and fail to thrive in a forest fragmented by freeways or condos. Dandelions don't care. Invading species are excellent indicators of environmental disturbance: the trashed river, the polluted lot. Like us, they are all-terrain creatures, unsympathetic to the specialists of the world: the orchids, the songbirds. As natives die back, opportunists like Japanese knotweed push in, rather as Manhattanites desperate for housing flip first to the obituary pages, sussing out which of the urban deceased has just vacated a nice rent-controlled apartment: prewar bldg w/doorman, fpl, 6 rms, sunny, riv view. Urban botanists are realists too, viewing all New York as one disconnected empty lot. Some of their best sightings happen in railroad rights of way, city landfills, stream shores, and backyard garden plots. (Brooklyn fire escapes and Bronx botanicas are especially thrilling, since human immigrants so often insist on bringing their favorite healing, beverage, and relaxing plants to America.)

Since modern civilization constantly propels plants and animals beyond their natural ranges into places they don't belong, some ecologists (and philosophers) have begun to argue, why *not* let nature take its course, with a little help from the jet age? Why so much prejudice against new-come species? Alien organisms alter ecosystems, but we don't know if that change is always for the worse. Mussels clog intake pipes, but they also make water cleaner, and attract wildfowl. Kudzu restores nitrogen to worn-out soil. The Asian swamp eels now loose in the Everglades are three feet long with razor teeth, but biologists would worry far more if the ecology of the Everglades were not already so corrupted that the impact of one more berserker species is nearly impossible to assess.

Do exotics upset the balance of nature? Profoundly, some scientists say. Richness (the number of types of species per area) and abundance (the number of species members on hand) equal diversity. The lower the species count, the more potential for disaster. Alien invasion is second only to habitat loss in depleting biodiversity, the planet's safety net—and ours. Diversity is good in a stock portfolio and even better in an environment. Diversity ensures that when the system is stressed—a drought, a disease, a rash of supermalls—whole communities of plants and animals won't be wiped out. And diversity, especially, prevents one species from turning bully and taking over a landscape. The McDonaldization of flora is acute these days; in North America alone, more than five thousand native species are at risk. Local solutions help: urban and suburban gardeners should think of their yards and flowerbeds as zoos, and guard against escapes; ship-ballast systems could be reengineered to screen for foreign plants and creatures; landscapers should hold out for native species, and be much more wary of exotics, which are often sold by nurseries as quick-fix or care-free. We are all our brothers' groundskeepers. Consider caulerpa, a feathery bright-green algae, specially bred by a German aquarium to dress up its saltwater displays. In the early 1980s, super-caulerpa samples went to aquariums in Japan, South Africa, France, and Monaco. Around 1984, a frond or two escaped into the open Mediterranean. A mismanaged biotic invasion became an environmental disaster as governments bickered while the invader spread, coating the sea floor and releasing toxins that kill local species—and commercial fishing, and sportfishing, and scuba sites, and pleasant beachfront living. Marine biologists report that the bottom of the northern Mediterranean, once one of the most complex and beautiful ecologies anywhere, now looks like AstroTurf, a desert of green. Early in 2000, some idiot in southern California dumped a fish tank into a storm drain, introducing caulerpa to United States waters north of San Diego.

Sentimental nonsense, other researchers retort. Don't look for pattern and cause in nature; there isn't any. Yes, the United States government has announced all-out war on exotic-species invaders, as well as on global diseases. But just how intensely do we want to manage the unmanageable? Persuading the public that crabgrass is a security risk will be tough enough, and may commit us to modern ecological Vietnams. Besides, ecosystems lack order, purpose, and design because they *have* no balance *to* disrupt, no stable set point, no equilibrium, only constant struggle. Such last-century metaphors need to go. Any environment is constantly in flux, a shimmer and foam of change across time and space.

Global warming has begun to render all sides moot, and mute. As the world heats up, plant and animal species are moving north at startling rates. Ohio already has palm trees. Thawing permafrost and a thinning ice pack are disrupting animal breeding and migration cycles across Alaska and upper Canada.

Nature is supremely practical. In New York, it eats sidewalks, not skyscrapers. Spurge is the first plant to soften an aging concrete slab, a sudden flourish of tiny green leaves with red chevrons. Then comes carpetweed, climbing the concrete edges. Grasses crack the weakened sidewalk. Water seeps in, freezes, then levers up slabs. Ants arrive, and beetles.

Naturalists observing one razed SoHo lot found that dozens of baby trees sprang up within five years—cottonwood, honey locust, willow, silver maple—all from seeds windborne, or birdborne, or carried into lower Manhattan on muddy tire treads or somebody's shoe sole. Coltsfoot, aster, chicory, Queen Anne's lace, plantain, mugwort, wild lettuce, and bindweed arrived the same way. About half of the SoHo plant pioneers observed were natives, half aliens. All exploited every edge, every niche. Decaying paper and cardboard dumped in the lot became impromptu compost. Discarded cement makes the soil alkaline, which clover and locust like. Rain collects in the mounds of dirty gravel; one leaky hydrant can save dozens of species. In half a decade, if such a lot is not scraped clean for a luxury highrise or a Gap outlet, it will look remarkably like New York after the last great glacier withdrew: gravelly rubble firmly colonized by a rush of green.

Leave a New York vacant lot alone for ten thousand years,

botanists proudly say, and you'll have a perfect little hardwood forest. The New York Botanical Garden, twenty minutes from Grand Central, still has forty acres of virgin timber, a mixed stand of hickories, oaks, maples, tulip trees, and hemlocks, many of them mature when George Washington was a boy. But the ashes and dogwoods in New York's last sizable wild forest are struggling, and the hemlocks are dying or dead, the cumulative legacy of road runoff, acid rain, and pollution from the Bronx River at the forest's edge.

Across town at the Brooklyn Botanic Garden, the heroic Metropolitan Flora Project (which plans to identify and catalog all trees, vines, shrubs, ferns, grasses, and flowers that grow within fifty miles of Times Square) has already docketed 2,750 plant species in Greater New York. But the lists of the vanished are nearly as impressive. Of the top 50 woody plants in the metro area, 13 are not native. In Queens alone, half of the native plant species have been killed off since the 1920s. On Staten Island, 40 percent are missing. It takes three or four hours for the Garden's volunteers and professionals to complete a plant census of a single city block. Linnaeus and Darwin would recognize the technique: the plant detectives take to the streets and write down every plant they see—a bio-blitz. Project news notes read like a police-precinct bulletin board, full of kudzu sightings, anemone alerts, virburnum escapes, and apparent suicide missions, like the hedge-maple seedlings found trying really, really hard to colonize an entrance ramp to the Brooklyn-Queens Expressway.

Botanists only nod, and make a note. They know that converting the BQE into a maple grove is what nature does best. Even in New York—maybe especially in New York—nature bats last. If you come to Manhattan's Pennsylvania Station by train, be sure to look up as the cars emerge from tunnel darkness and begin to slow. The first thing a city visitor sees is a five-story abutment, cracked from top to bottom by honey locust trees, growing calmly out of the concrete wall.

Morningside Heights is a Manhattan neighborhood built on cliffs of mica schist, overlooking Harlem to the east and the Hudson River to the west. Grant's Tomb is there, and the gravely elegant Beaux Arts campus of Columbia University, but the skyline belongs to the massive Episcopalian Cathedral of Saint John the Divine at Amsterdam Avenue and 112th Street, half Romanesque, half Gothic, and perpetually unfinished. Each October, the cathedral observes the Feast of Saint Francis of Assisi by holding a special service to honor this thirteenth-century Italian sophisticate turned social radical, a friend to wolves and sheep alike, who warned against the overstuffed life, claiming that each of us is a lute string strung for rapture, but only if we want everything and expect nothing. The Saint Francis liturgy is one of New York's few formal tributes to the wild, and a very hot ticket: admission is free, but the line for the service forms at dawn. Afterward, in the cathedral garden, clergy provide individual pet blessings. Over the years, staffers have sanctified a turkey vulture, a skunk, a tarantula, a bowl of worms, a billion-year-old Australian fossil, and quite a few teddy bears.

Long before the Earth Mass begins, the cathedral starts to fill. Five thousand people will attend the service, which has become as popular as the Christmas and Easter celebrations. Among the rows of small hard chairs, animals are everywhere.

Two Irish setters in matching Aran sweaters sniff at a King Charles spaniel in a brown spandex raincoat. A black standard poodle and an elderly pug roll blissfully against a pillar. A Skye terrier, collared in red pom-poms, barks with happiness at the nearness of so many other New York dogs. Beside me, a brace of unhappy Siamese huddle in their cat carrier, making sarcastic comments. A passing Akita snuggles a cold wet nose into my hand. The animals bear names like Zach and Colette, Eudora and Ramsey, Tuli and Eames. The Upper West Side fauna escorting them (variously clad in saris, turtlenecks, Guatemalan ponchos, vintage Chanel, and battered tweed, but no fur coats) trade air kisses and ecumenical hugs, then raptly discuss dog-play groups, dog-therapy options, dog carbo-loading diets, and special dog CDs of animal sounds.

New York can have odd effects on pets. Cats lose depth perception and fall out of apartment windows so regularly that vets have a name for it: high-building syndrome. Dogs suffer terribly from constipation; unable to see grass or sky when walking down the street, they often decide that New York is one big room. Both species frequently experience free-floating urban anxiety, for which vets recommend Xanax, or Prozac—sometimes for the animals, sometimes for the owners. Today the humans in the cathedral are overexcited and the animals dignified, despite heavy odds. A burly Maine coon cat, panting with stress in its owner's arms, is patted by cooing strangers; spaniels and ferrets and lop-eared rabbits are carried by, all wearing outsized wreaths of plastic daisies. A tall, lean black man with a boa constrictor wound round his neck edges politely past. The great serpent's chain-mail scales gleam in the blue light of the rose window, high in the vaulted transept.

As the hour for the processional nears, a battery of theatrical lighting illuminates the crossing, and dancers in white gauze pajamas dash importantly about as the dean of the cathedral helps the congregation practice arm motions for the opening hymn. "Be like beautiful waving wheat," he tells the crowd, "and let the children do and be what children do and be. Let the pets do and be what pets do and be . . . within reason."

Dancers whirl up the aisles toward the high altar, waving sea-green ribbons to a burst of percussion, and the clergy follow, glittering in embroidered copes. The Episcopal Bishop of New York keeps a liver-spotted setter on a tight leash as the cathedral fills with the sharp scents of liturgical incense, damp dog, and damp stone. The audio director cues a tape of timber-wolf cries, and all through the nave, dogs and children throw back their heads and reply. Someone is reading the program over my shoulder—no, two someones: an elderly Hispanic gentleman in a London Fog raincoat and a noble spiked and scaly green iguana, two feet long, riding calmly on his shoulder.

Nature is nondenominational, the sermon argues. In northern California, a coalition of rabbis is protesting the clear-cutting of ancient forest. America's Catholic bishops have issued a pastoral letter on the importance of preserving the Columbia River's wild and scenic qualities. And evangelicals are flocking to the stewardship movement: since Genesis commands us not only to subdue the earth but to guard it well, right-of-center Protestants have begun to mix conservative theology and environmental action, plus congressional sit-ins.

"Jews in the redwoods, Catholics in the rivers, born-agains defending endangered species: we in this Episcopal congregation can seem a bit tame. Perhaps Francis will lead us, as patron saint of both ecology and justice, without which ecology is only natural science. Sin is conceit, and the greatest human conceit is to forget that all life is connected. We need an ecumenical strategy that integrates, heals, and makes whole, for scientists tell us that independence in the biosphere is always death-dealing."

In the shadowy side aisles, stilt-walking Caribbean mocko jumbies stride past. More dancers pirouette in their wake, flourishing green and gold banners, impersonating a school of whales. In the transept, a major dog fight breaks out. For humans, the Feast of Saint Francis is a combination of NPR, Mardi Gras, and a seminar in world religions, a celebration of nature in a cold, dark, intensely theatrical space. The animal-eye view is perhaps less satisfying: many thousand humans, pressing close and singing loudly, a cold stone floor, strange ankles and strange muzzles, drums and more drums.

I slip out the side door into the damp, soft October morning to join the crowds on Amsterdam Avenue. Hundreds watch, enchanted, as the final Procession of the Animals assembles behind police lines. All the animal handlers wear scarlet cassocks, and many of their charges, for the moment, roam free. The elephant who usually leads is out sick, but subbing for her is a splendid camel wreathed in green—a union camel, from a theatrical supplier in Connecticut. Behind the camel waits a pale-gray ox, wide-horned; a neurotic llama, shying at the traffic; and a somnolent donkey. Penguins hop up and down the broad cathedral steps until firmly tucked under a penguin wrangler's arm. Two teenage handlers balance a flat hive of bees. A pair of silver tabbies stalk a hefty white rabbit while the oblivious handlers chat, and a midsize tortoise with a nosegay scotch-taped to his shell makes a slow break for the Hudson River, four blocks west. Other handlers deftly manage a great horned owl, a monkey, a struggling weasel, and a handsome spotted goat. Cassocked grade-schoolers hold up hamsters, a potbellied piglet, a goldfish bowl.

All along Amsterdam Avenue, urban animal lovers have begun hauling pet carriers out of the backseats of taxicabs, ready to claim a postservice blessing in the cathedral close. Passing New Yorkers stop, crane over the police barricades, then anthropomorphize with enthusiasm.

"Look, that one, he's saying, 'Let's get *out* of here!' "

"And *she* say, 'I'm gonna *eat* you, sucker!' "

The head wrangler, talking urgently into a headset, gestures the full procession into line. Flashbulbs leap to life. "Awww," says the crowd, watching them go. Even the police say "Awww" as the cathedral's bronze doors swing open, and the birds of the air and the beasts of the field, every living thing, move slowly out of the pale autumn light into the crowded cave of stone, with arched necks and extended wings.

Afterward, in the garden, the nonsectarian blessings commence and, more gingerly, the laying on of hands, though clergy are almost never bitten or scratched on blessing day. The same prayers fit chihuahuas and chipmunks, turtles and tarantulas:

Maker of all living creatures;
you called forth fish in the sea
birds in the air and animals on the land.
You inspired Saint Francis to call all animals
his brothers and sisters.

We ask you to bless this animal;
enable it to live according to your plan.

I lay my hands upon you in the name of the one
    Creator.
O Lord, we ask your blessing upon . . .
this fine gerbil, Gus—
this parrot, Maxine—
this beloved goldfish, Fish—
this snake, Jake—you're holding him nice and tight?
    Okay, then—
this golden retriever—
this *extremely lively* kitten—

New York definitions of *domestic pet* can be elastic. Six adult
alligators were once found living in a Brooklyn brownstone.
Manhattan renters have left behind pythons in apartment bath-
tubs. An illegal rooster was recently arrested in the Bronx,
mostly because it insisted on greeting the dawn, a violation of
city noise ordinances. New York specifically bans 150 animals
from urban residency, including armadillos, iguanas, vultures,
prairie dogs, black widow spiders, Tasmanian devils, kangaroos,
pythons, ferrets, and whales. But at the Feast of Saint Francis,
more than a few fugitive ferrets and outlaw iguanas, kept prudently under their owners' coats until the crucial moment,
nonetheless received a proper blessing. No arrests were made.
The boundary between domestic and wild, sacred and profane,
remains open to negotiation. The ancient custom of sanctuary
holds.

Deep Time in the Bronx

Cismontane southern California, the busy coastal strip from San Diego to Santa Barbara, contains perhaps one-sixteenth of the Golden State's land mass, and half its population. California's eight Channel Islands form a long archipelago beside this crowded left coast. Some are eleven miles offshore, others sixty. The largest is Santa Cruz, an island three times the size of Manhattan with a year-round population of eleven. Almost no one goes there, except scientists and backpackers. Getting to Santa Cruz means a two-hour boat ride from Santa Barbara, or else a chartered flight from the Camarillo airport to Santa Cruz International, which has no runway, no schedule, and no guarantees, only a very small plane threading past sheer cliffs and sea lion rookeries, followed by a sudden plunge toward a cow-pasture landing at the Pacific's edge, as cloud shadows race over the folded drapery of the lion-colored hills.

Santa Cruz is an island of microclimates, ranged around a narrow central valley. Veils of waterfall brighten the sun-beaten live-oak canyons. Ironwood groves, extinct now on the mainland, are loud with ravens and island jays. Cloud forests of wind-stunted pine yield to mountain passes with hundred-mile views. Santa Cruz is rugged, but not pristine. The Chumash tribes that lived and fished here were displaced by Spanish sheep ranchers, who sold the land to Franco-Italian vintners. A clan of wealthy Los Angelenos used the island as a summer preserve until deeding most of it to the Nature Conservancy. Unsurprisingly, Santa Cruz is full of naturalized species, from Australian eucalyptus to the gray-violet scrim of European fennel on valley hillsides. "The weeds really run the place," say the reserve managers, sighing.

They're so right: the Nature Conservancy, the Parks Service, and the University of California at Santa Barbara all help maintain Santa Cruz, but their visions of its future conflict. Thus it remains an island of failed farms and feral fennel, a landscape of intensive disturbance that only looks wild. Winery, cattle ranch, sheep farm, silent-movie lot—the island defeated all. Feral pigs are everywhere, fierce and omnivorous, rototilling the soil with trotters and snouts in search of lily bulbs and grubs. Except for the pigs, which have been on their own since 1850, and a remnant designer herd of polled Herefords at the historic main ranch, the Nature Conservancy is slowly erasing all evidence of human habitation from Santa Cruz, to the despair of visiting botanists and biologists and ornithologists and entomologists (who want to do science, or at least practice salvage biology), and the intense irritation of the Parks Service, which would rather encourage head counts and concessions stands to bring over more campers and day-trippers.

For the moment, Santa Cruz Island is one of the loneliest places in the lower forty-eight, and immensely quiet, except for the wind in the manzanita, the surf, and the golden eagles (new and successful predators, commuting from the mainland), who call to one another as they patrol the rose and tan mountainsides, hunting the tiny, graceful island foxes. Island nights are wild indeed. Sometimes you can see the reflected glow of L.A., fifty miles south. On the landward face, at Prisoners' Harbor, a haze of town lights marks the foothills of the snow-covered Coastal Range. The halogen searchbeams of Japanese squid boats sometimes rake the sky to the west. But mostly, the island night is illuminated only by the Milky Way, wheeling above the hills, and the darkness is loud with the sounds of mating and eating. A dead island pig left at roadside simply isn't there in the morning; the other pigs devour it. Nothing is left but a stain. On an island, Darwinian processes are distilled and magnified. There is nowhere else to go. This is *it*. Work it out, or die.

Biologists love islands because interaction and layering there are brutally simple, as opposed to mainland muddle. The essence of an island is not necessarily that it is isolated, but that it is discrete, with severely limited habitat. Ceaseless competition for resources means ceaseless pressure to adapt, which is why islands (and islanders) are tough, and continents relatively fragile. The more hostile an island environment, the more rigorous the standards for passing Go; islands are perfect laboratories for making survivor species identify themselves, as New Yorkers, human and non-, have demonstrated for centuries.

So: islands intensify. Islands also accumulate. Once something is on-island, whether artifact or life-form, you can't get it off without enormous trouble. Studying the collection of vintage trucks and harrows and rusted bedsprings behind the

Santa Cruz cookhouse, I thought suddenly of my Fifth Avenue walk to work down the spine of Manhattan, where every leaf and stone and artifact has been imported too—the mango fizz and the chanterelle mushrooms, the Sheraton breakfronts and the fourteenth-century psalters, the marble stair treads and the limestone embrasures, the orchids, the ottomans, the Jimmy Choo stilettos, the number-two pencils, the taxis and the taxi medallions, the air filters, the mops, the MasterCard receipts, the cat chow—all laboriously shipped in from the American mainland, as the island city's garbage, with the closing of Fresh Kills, must all be laboriously shipped back, then sent by train and truck to landfills in Idaho and Virginia.

When the scientists and reserve managers of Santa Cruz meet for dinner after a day of ant counts and butterfly genetics, their early talk is of interspecies tips, from the best ways to lure island foxes into banding traps (use liver pâté on dog biscuits, or else fruit roll-ups) to what to do when sea lions sneak up and nibble at your flippers (don't kick). Santa Cruz has only four native mammals—the island fox, two kinds of mice, and the jaunty island skunks, which like to sleep behind the water heater in the science-station outhouse, long striped tails sticking out of the insulation. Like their Galapagos counterparts, Santa Cruz animals are often friendly toward humans, or at least polite. It's their island. But as the evening spins out, the scientists begin to talk of what-ifs, and the power of contingency, and the counterfactual past. Biologists and geologists love puzzles, last stands, and dead ends that aren't: What if the Spanish Armada had triumphed? Or Napoleon at Waterloo? Or Robert E. Lee at Gettysburg?

I remember their passion for other pasts the next day, when jeep-touring a series of lost outranches. The island won here too. The nineteenth-century barns and bunkhouses are faint ruins of stone and adobe overgrown by sage scrub, and the market roads have shrunk to merest tracks running toward a whitecapped Pacific, where other Channel Islands ride the ocean haze beneath a midafternoon moon. Metallic-green beetles wander outcrops of white Monterey shale; violet-blue lupine and creamy mariposa lilies, veined and rimmed in purple, bend under the sea wind; western meadowlarks carol. Santa Cruz is itself a counterfactual island, harboring fragments of the California of 1890, and 1800, and more than a bit of 1600. Early California was a scene of unparalleled, almost unimaginable, natural richness. Today it is the state with the most endangered species. But Santa Cruz Island, for all its record of human interference, is also a last link to the wondrous California that Cortez and Francis Drake knew. If their settlement plans had succeeded, the Atlantic seaboard would be our unspoiled shore. We would romanticize the Everglades and the wild Smokies. Katahdin would be our Yosemite, and New York Bay a national park. If the United States had been settled west to east, Santa Cruz Island would have been long since terraformed into parking lots and skyscrapers, and Manhattan would be the nature reserve. And if Peter Minuit and the Dutch West India Company had picked Staten Island for their main trading fort, all New York today might be as tidy and lowrise a capital as London or Stockholm or Paris. Environmentally speaking, Manhattan has always been unsuited to heavy settlement.

For most students of the past, nature is historical wallpaper, not the main event. But the natural world—snow and granite, roaches and cholera—deserves a more prominent place in the collective stories we call history. A civilian walking through Central Park may stop to admire an outcrop of dark rock the size of a city bus, watch ice skaters on the big pond at the park's north end, then visit Strawberry Fields, the John Lennon memorial mosaic near Seventy-second Street. Central Park's lampposts are discreetly numbered, to help birders pinpoint unusual sightings, and the Great Lawn is a superb public space for people watching, concerts, pickup soccer, and Ultimate Frisbee.

An environmental historian will walk the same route and see a different park and a different New York, forcing the view wider, deeper, longer, wilder. The outcrops of mica schist near Central Park South are good for climbing, but they're also the eroded nubs of an ancient mountain range that once rose higher than the Alps. Harlem Meer, like Central Park's other ponds, was thoroughly redesigned in the 1800s to look more romantic and unkempt. Engineers carefully imported boulders and piped in artificial waterfalls. Ostrich ferns and skunk cabbage, thought to be the area's original streambed vegetation, were only recently reintroduced. Like most of today's Upper West Side, the Strawberry Fields area was once malarial marsh and poison-ivy thicket, inhabited by semiferal pigs. Park bird habitat used to be exurban human habitat. Sixteen hundred Irish and German shantytown residents were displaced to build Central Park, and an African-American settlement called Seneca Village (a substantial place, with three churches and a school) was entirely demolished. The Great Lawn recently required an $18 million rehab to make it look natural again. Twenty-five thousand cubic yards of sand and brewery by-products, trucked in from Long Island, formed a base for Connecticut sod, a mix of perennial rye and five different Kentucky bluegrasses. (Bluegrass is really English timothy, used in straw form by pioneers to protect their trade goods. When the seed arrived on this continent, it escaped the packs, sprouted, and thrived.) Beneath the lawn lies an 1847 storm sewer, but also the Lower Croton Receiving Reservoir, a manmade aquifer filled with 1930s rubble left over from the construction of Rockefeller Center. Three million people a year use the Great Lawn, as many as visit Yellowstone.

The Western tradition sets in opposition nature and culture, city and wilderness, capital and provinces, enclosed garden and unmapped forest. But until very recently, as the environmental historian Donald Worster observes, almost all people lived as intimately with other species and with wind and weather as with their own kind. To restore nature as agent and presence in history, we need to get out more—out of parliamentary chambers, out of birthing rooms and factories—and ramble in the open air. Not everyone agrees. Making nature the main character in history devalues the human spirit, traditionalists complain. Nature is a figment of the imagination, a mere cultural construction, argue the theory-minded. Nature is a bad career move, many scholars whisper; professionally speaking, indoor-history fields like diplomacy or politics are high-status, outdoor topics like maritime or agricultural history distinctly pleb. New York history often tries to get inside as fast as possible, stay there, and order in.

But the advance of the natural city makes it smart—adaptive, even—to remember that New York is a city founded in an atypical interval of good weather, an inter–Ice Age, and to keep

in mind that the paving of its many islands replicates in miniature the planet's ongoing sixth mass extinction. Historians of
science know that we of the early twenty-first century are wit-
nesses to the largest dieback of plants and animals in sixty-five
million years. The last mass extinction was caused by a giant
meteorite strike near present-day Yucatan, which ended the age
of dinosaurs. The current extinction is anthropogenic: caused
by us.

The last great glacier to visit New York was a thousand feet
thick, a sloping wall of dirty ice as tall as today's skyline, except
for the very tip of the Empire State Building and the tops of
the World Trade towers. It slid south as far as Brooklyn and
Queens, halted near the present location of the Statue of Liberty, and stayed. Seventeen thousand years ago, as the glacier
retreated, its meltwater pooled into giant inland lakes—Lake
Passaic, Lake Hackensack. The Ice Age was good to New York,
creating one of the world's great harbors, deep yet sheltered,
and it scoured the area flat, leaving a bare-rock platform where
a city might grow. The first of the three major rock types that
underlie New York is a dark fire-born gneiss, dove-gray to
thundercloud-gray, folded and twisted, a billion years old. A
slightly younger coarse pale marble overlies it, and the mica
schist of the Manhattan formation, which sparkles on the fa-
cades of some older city buildings, can be seen in raw form
beside the Cross Bronx Expressway. It also provides the
weathered outcrops of Central Park. The same durable schist
supports the towers of midtown, but then vanishes underground for many blocks to emerge again in the financial district,

which is why the New York skyline soars, then dips, then soars once more at the island's south tip: Greenwich Village and Chelsea are built on soil, but the center of Manhattan Island is solid granite, like its southern end. (Even so, scientists at the Museum of Natural History think the city's bedrock may have begun to bend under such tremendous construction weight.)

For thousands of years, postglacial New York looked like northern Alaska, a treeless tundra of mosses and lichens. Then it looked like Manitoba, a landscape of swamp and peat bog, and then like coastal Maine, all spruce and meadows. Subway construction sometimes brings to light the skeletons of former New York residents, such as saber-toothed tigers and giant sloths, and sometimes releases the gemstones beneath the city—rose quartz and garnet and amethyst and aquamarine. (Geologists afoot in New York also spot corals from Morocco in the polished marble walls of Wall Street lobbies, and note tiny fossils in the limestone sills of Tiffany's Fifth Avenue display windows.)

As a warming climate drove the last New York bear and caribou north, the ocean rose once more, drowning coastal valleys to make rivers, inlets, more islands. Hardwood forests of hickory and oak began to thrive. Human hunters may have arrived twelve thousand years ago, maybe thirty thousand; archaeologists are still fighting it out. But from about A.D. 1400 on, a branch of the Delaware tribes called the Lenape kept seasonal hunting and farming camps in the New York area. Up to sixty thousand lived between central Connecticut and mid–New Jersey. They built longhouses, traveled an island hunting trail that Europeans later renamed the Broad Way, and practiced slash-and-burn agriculture; the lush meadows and cathedral-like woodlands so admired here in the years of Europeans' first contact owed much to Lenape land management.

European land scouts came looking for profit, not scenery, and certainly not revelation. But the mere smell of the place clearly haunted them. When a seventeenth-century wind from the American coast met you ten miles out to sea, a heart-lifting fragrance apparently rode with it—sweet, healthy, bracing, better than sun-warmed laundry, richer than a fresh-cut lawn, the scent of three thousand miles of blossoming continent. Until it faded, about the time of the Revolution, Dutch adventurers, English accountants, Swedish naturalists, and French clergy struggled in vain to describe the American air. Travelers marveled nearly as much at the bountiful countryside and crystalline water of early New York: the place is a wonder, they said. An Eden, a Canaan.

The Dutch trading port of New Amsterdam was founded in 1626, at the tip of the long narrow island the Lenape called Manahatta. Colonists' letters tell of six-foot lobsters and foot-long oysters, vast tangles of blackberries and raspberries, and wild turkeys tame enough to be caught by hand. The coastal rocks were dark with seals, whales played in Long Island Sound, and when the local wild swans settled in a meadow to rest and feed, it looked like a summer snowfall. "There are some people who imagine that the animals of the country will be destroyed in time," wrote an early colonist, Adriaen van der Donck, "but this is an unnecessary anxiety." He was an optimist: suppressing nature meant a healthier bottom line. By 1640, the Europeans were already altering the island, trimming the rocky shoreline into neat commercial anchorages and adding piers near Wall and Pearl Streets, named respectively for the wooden palisade that kept out wild animals and for the gleaming middens left by years of Lenape oyster feasts.

New York was one of the earliest European ventures to secure its East Coast foothold. The city is older than Williamsburg, younger than St. Augustine, and much, much younger than the urban centers far to the Southwest—the Pueblo villages of the mesas, already established for centuries, or the royal Spanish city of Santa Fe. The Dutch West India Company was like Exxon with guns, observes New York historian Mike Wallace; it already controlled the global Asian spice trade, and had begun to experiment, not very hard, with company towns in the Americas, from Brazil up to Manhattan. Beaver and otter skins were essential to the European fashion industry, so the shabby frontier fort on the Hudson was a low-risk try at challenging the French monopoly on New World furs. It worked; by 1650, the local deer and bear were hunted out, and eighteen languages were being spoken in Manhattan, a polyglot tradition that continued without a break when the British took over the lease in 1664 and renamed the outpost New York.

New York was the only Atlantic American colony not English in origin. Unlike Massachusetts and Rhode Island, it was not a spiritual or social experiment; unlike Virginia, it felt no need to maintain the dressing-for-dinner-in-the-jungle ethos of British colonies from Tasmania to Calcutta. The global-trading Dutch designed New York as a tolerant free port. From the first, it was considered bad for business to exclude *anyone*. The town absorbed cultures and information and cash like a wetland soaks up water. True, the local tolerance proved in practice to be formal rather than warm, and the rich-poor split was always marked, like the local self-absorption, and the local mouth.

(Said an indignant John Adams a century later: "[New Yorkers] talk very loud, very fast, and altogether. If they ask you a question, before you utter three words of your answer, they will break out upon you again and talk away.")

On June 3, 1776, the citizens of New York awoke to find their town invaded; the British government had sent a massive war fleet to subdue rebellion in the Empire's third-largest port. "I was upstairs," wrote a young American soldier stationed in Brooklyn, "and spied as I peeped out at the Bay something resembling a wood of pine trees, trimmed . . . I thought all London was afloat." The military and environmental histories of New York converged that summer at America's Dunkirk, when a heavy night fog descended after the disastrous Battle of Brooklyn, allowing Washington to evacuate his entire army across the East River in seven hours, without a casualty and without a sound, to escape up the wooded length of Manhattan and fight on. Without that lucky bit of New York weather, many historians believe, Americans might still speak in British accents.

The New York Commissioner's Plan looked insane when released in 1811—a waffle-iron grid projecting commercial development all the way to the island's north end, a two days' ride away. Only Broadway was still allowed to meander in this relentlessly rational vision of New York's future. Forcing disorderly New York to physically evolve into a moneymaking machine was an act of great economic hubris (particularly since present-day SoHo marked the outer edge of town) and great environmental defiance. The grid simply ignored Manhattan's many hills, streams, and swamps, rather as the city's merchants and inventors were ignoring geography, space, and time, first with Robert Fulton's steamboat, launched from a Greenwich Village dock in 1807, and then with the 1818 advent of the New York–based Black Ball line, which invented both the shipping schedule and the phrase "on-time delivery." After 1825, the Erie Canal linked the Hudson to the West, making New York the key point of American entry. The energized merchant city leapfrogged north, gobbling land, filling in the grid. "Could I begin life again, knowing what I know now," said the aged fur trader John Jacob Astor, the nation's richest man, "I would buy every foot of land on the island of Manhattan."

By 1840, New York invented the phrase "traffic jam," and well-off Manhattanites turned nostalgic for the greener, quainter, more homogenous city their grandparents knew. They rushed to rustic resorts in summer, trying to ease stress with scenery, and bought the Fenimore Cooper novels and Thomas Cole paintings that glorified a lost eastern wilderness, now fragmented into edge habitat by clear-cutting and train tracks. But through bank panics and boom times, the antebellum city packed more and more bodies into the same limited terrain. Real estate prices rose shockingly. The rich found relief in private parks like Gramercy; the poor had rooftops, and the street. The shoreline disappeared too, replaced by a Manhattan "belted about with wharves," as New Yorker Herman Melville observed in 1854. "Circumnambulate the city on a dreamy Sabbath afternoon. What do you see? —Posted like silent sentinels all around the town, stand thousands upon thousands of mortal men . . . some seated on the pier heads, some looking over the bulwarks of ships. These are all landsmen; of weekdays pent up in lath and plaster—tied to counters, nailed to benches, clinched to desks. How then is this? Are the green fields gone?"

Leaf and Stone

Manhattan before the Civil War was an industrial island of factories, mills, garment sweatshops, shipyards, and foundries, rich in civic novelties like a professional police force, a public transit system of horse-drawn streetcars all the way to semirural Harlem, and a new marketing craze, the department store (wildly popular, and open late, thanks to the new gas lighting, which replaced the traditional whale-oil lamps, ending a global industry and giving the world's thoroughly endangered whales some chance at recovery). Yet well into the nineteenth century, large American cities like New York relied on immigration to keep population levels steady, since urban diseases killed so many residents each week. By 1840, horse manure and raw sewage slicked New York pavements. Garbage rose uncollected in gutters and vacant lots, defeating even the efforts of the local pigs, the city's sole street cleaners. Only the poor dared to use city water pumps. Germ theory was in its infancy; leading physicians recommended cayenne pepper, mothballs, syrup of opium, and moral reform as sure preventatives for malaria, yellow fever, and the dreaded cholera, which arrived in North America with the immigrant ships of the early 1830s.

The cholera years—1832, 1849, and 1866—killed perhaps one-tenth of New York, especially in slums like Five Points, where the newly arrived Irish lived in conditions described by one young doctor as worse than any endured by the worst-treated slaves of his native South. Crowding made infection swift, and half a million people were packed into the tenements below Twenty-third Street. Blaming immigrants for the epidemics was easier than reforming Manhattan's plumbing (as late as 1857, New York provided sewers for barely one-fifth of its streets), but the spectacle of thousands of rats swimming to the city cemeteries on Randall's Island to eat the dead finally forced the city to act. Health standards remained a civic weakness until well after the Civil War, and not only in the low-rent districts; Theodore Roosevelt's mother, Mittie, died of typhoid in her Fifty-seventh Street townhouse in 1884, the victim of contaminated food or water.

A twenty-first-century visitor to mid-nineteenth-century New York would immediately notice how empty the skies were, how busy the waters, how modest the skyline. Commuter ferries, steam yachts, paddlewheelers churning upriver to Albany, three-masted barques bringing immigrants to Ellis Island, clippers of the China trade, and early transatlantic liners, all came and went from a fiendishly crowded but low-rise city. Though the first demonstration of the safety elevator was held in New York in 1853, its first true skyscraper, the dramatic freestanding tower of the Flatiron Building, had to wait until 1902, when steel-frame construction was perfected. In the years between, lower Manhattan slums reached a density of six hundred people per acre—worse than Calcutta—while upper Manhattan experimented with a new style of respectable domesticity, the city apartment building.

But above all, in that other New York, we would notice the smell: of rotting fish guts, overflowing outhouses, boiled cabbage, dead horse, and unwashed neighbor. In 1858, London endured the Great Stink. A hot summer turned sewage in the Thames so noxious that Parliament hung burlap soaked in chloride of lime over House of Commons windows, and hastily passed a serious public-sanitation law. In New York, every day was a Great Stink, with two results: development got serious about moving outward, especially after the East River inconveniently froze solid in 1867, locking the Manhattan-Brooklyn ferries in ice but giving ambitious engineers the idea for the Brooklyn Bridge; and New Yorkers began to notice that nature, sufficiently provoked, bites back—a two-century New York institution, the fresh-oyster bar, was becoming extinct. New York's local oysters were famously sweet and briny, and city gourmands needed only one bite to identify the varieties: Cold Spring, Cow Bay, Oyster Bay, or the massive Saddle Rock, large as a man's hand. Rich and poor devoured them raw, fried, stewed, or scalloped, as street food and banquet fare. But by 1880, pollution and overdredging killed the wondrous native beds, forcing New Yorkers to eat imports from New England and Chesapeake Bay.

The five boroughs-to-be had, as yet, little in common. Gilded Age Manhattan bristled with high-life money and low-life crime; even the police kept out of certain downtown neighborhoods, and a popular ladies' gift item was the small enameled derringer, for purse or pocket. Brooklyn, safely across the river, was a great city in its own right, house-proud and church-proud, wreathed in neat, rich farmland. Staten Island was an early Hamptons, part artist's colony, part summer retreat for the well-to-do. Queens was potato farms. The Bronx (named for its early Scandinavian settler Jonas Bronk) seemed as remote from the life of the city as Texas. Manhattan alone lacked public green space. But The Central Park, begun in 1862, refashioned a rectangular tract just north of town into a collection of groves, meadows, ponds, and pleasure drives as conscientiously picturesque as a Hudson River School canvas. To blast the swampy, rocky landscape into order required more gunpowder than was used at the Battle of Gettysburg. The fin-

ished park was ridiculously large, said critics, a waste of potential commercial space. To designers Olmsted and Vaux, it trans-
lated democratic ideas into trees and dirt, providing a garden
for the middle classes and a safety valve for the slums. Like
Hyde Park and the Vienna Woods, Central Park and its Brooklyn cousin, Prospect Park, were examples of *rus in urbe:* nature
imported and improved as theater and therapy.

In March 1888, the greatest winter storm of the nineteenth
century hit New York with fifty-four straight hours of snow.
Trains and shipping ceased during the Blizzard of '88, thirty-
foot drifts choked the streets, gas and electricity were cut off,
and a dozen citizens froze to death. That spring, the trauma-
tized city resolved to bury its utility lines and build a subway.
Within four years of the system's 1904 debut, Interborough
Rapid Transit, today's IRT, carried one million passengers a day.
You could travel the expanding city from end to end for a
nickel, making the subway a great social leveler and public edu-
cator. The subway gave New Yorkers new access to woods and
shore and freed them to live in cheaper, greener Brooklyn and
Queens.

In 1898, Manhattan swallowed its suburbs. The city of
Greater New York was born, an amalgamation of Queens,
Brooklyn, Staten Island, and (*primus inter pares*) Manhattan.
Only London was larger. The Bronx held out till 1914, and
Brooklyn had second thoughts almost immediately, but could
not renege. Staten Island, a half hour from Manhattan by ferry,
kept an air of rural self-sufficiency the longest, but Queens and
Brooklyn were easy prey for development. In 1880, they were
the nation's second-most-productive vegetable farms, feeding
the city with ease; by 1919 their fields grew only suburbs, and

New York imported cheap southern produce via refrigerated railcars. Infilling of swamps and marshland to support rail tracks and highways continued to distort Manhattan's original shape, a trend that would accelerate with the new century. (The FDR Drive is built on rubble from the London Blitz, carried here as troopship ballast. Battery Park City, like San Francisco's Marina district, is entirely fill.) Sewage and garbage in the urban rivers noticeably increased—but why worry about water quality if you're no longer eating local shad and oysters?

By 1900, New York was the nation's corporate, media, entertainment, and banking headquarters. A thousand commuter trains a day traveled to the city from its new second-ring suburbs in New Jersey, Long Island, Connecticut, and the Hudson River Valley. A subway line reached the Bronx in 1904, kicking off extreme development there. By 1913, Pennsylvania Station and Grand Central Terminal at last linked New York to continental America by rail. As tenements and apartment housing spread to all the boroughs, the New York city core grew too—straight up, and very fast. A coherent zoning law appeared in 1916, the nation's first, requiring setbacks from the street to preserve urban light and air, and with its passage the modern New York skyline began to blossom, thanks to fast elevators plus high steel—plus air-conditioning.

After 1911, the Folies Bergère and the new movie palaces started to offer patrons "refrigerated air," ending the theater custom of shutting down in summer. The air-cooled office and the encapsulating auto made New Yorkers among the first Americans to move and work and live in a genuinely new environment. Deep porches, high ceilings, and thick walls disappeared from urban architects' vocabularies. Midtown's old livery stable district became the Great White Way, equally bright at midnight and noon, and loud with the horns of the new horseless taxicabs. By 1919, a city flirting with gridlock invested in a new invention, automatic traffic lights, installed in ornate bronze stanchions topped with little statues of Mercury, god of speed. New York drivers were not always clear on the color codes—red to come forward? green to turn?—but auto ownership quintupled.

By 1920, the film industry has left New York: not enough nature is left to satisfy the cameras. Intense twenties development continues the population shift to the suburbs and outer boroughs, as tiny, tidy houses fill the last of Brooklyn's sandy outwash plain—Bensonhurst, Flatbush, Bushwick—and Queens evolves completely from farmland to middle-class garden apartments. By the late 1920s, ticker-tape parades for aviators and sports heroes are the city's favorite blizzards, but something else disturbs the urban air as well; government officials notice that air pollution has cut the New York sunlight by half.

Close calls and alternate futures begin to trouble New York's forward rush. On the eve of the stock-market crash, a private group of moneymen and developers release their Regional Plan, proposing a high-rise, high-speed future for a New York they believe might someday spread over twenty-two counties and three states. Their vision of a rail-linked, slum-pruned supercity is as daring as the 1811 commissioner's grid, and as business-driven. Had the Depression not intervened, all of lower Manhattan would probably have been subjected to its proposed Art Deco makeover. Instead, the first Depression years find citydwellers sleeping in the parks, and the city prudently evacuates the last few sheep in the Sheep Meadow, for fear that hungry New Yorkers will eat them. New Deal money brings playgrounds and open spaces, clinics and airports. But the urban personality splits more than a bit, the seedy, vivid, utterly capitalist city against a wholesomely reformed one, full of hygiene, social work, and regulation. Government action at all levels begins to shape New York like a gardener snipping unruly topiary. The city's great planning czar Robert Moses spends the thirties tearing apart established neighborhoods in order to tie together Greater New York with new green space, more tunnels and bridges, and a net of arterial highways that tilt the city definitively toward a car-and-truck future. (Even today, New York, not Los Angeles, has the most miles of urban highway.)

In the late 1940s, factory and blue-collar jobs—trucking, wholesale, shipping, manufacturing—will peak in the five boroughs. Newark and Stamford are clean, prosperous cities; New Jersey really is the Garden State; and 96 percent of New Yorkers tell the Gallup poll, in these halcyon years, that they are "happy" or "very happy." Unless, of course, they make a wrong turn. "Anyone who doubts that American civilization is industrial has only to take a train from New York to Philadelphia or, better yet, get lost driving in the Newark-Jersey City area, underneath the Pulaski Skyway," wrote a shaken John Gunther in 1947. "Here the fangs of industry really bite. There is not a blade of grass, if one may exaggerate slightly, in a dozen square miles. In a small car, at dusk, as the giant trucks and trailers grind their way through loops in smeary roads, one feels like a grasshopper caught in a stampede of iron elephants. The whole area is a kind of demonic metal shambles." Nor should you swim in postwar New York waterways, like Gerritsen Creek or the Gowanus Canal. Conscripted as factory sewers for decades, metal dipped in their foul waters visibly corrodes. Anything organic simply dissolves, and sinks into the lightless depths.

By the mid-1950s, spotting even a small wild animal in Manhattan merits a story in *The New York Times*, as when an opossum is captured by police in Washington Heights, "in glorious battle with nine alley cats." The city retains a few foxes in the Bronx, a few woodchucks in Queens. To see deer, try the zoo. For bears, Yosemite. (In the industrialized nations, you can see the air too. A Pennsylvanian coal-country smog in 1948 kills 20 and hospitalizes 6,000. In 1952, 4,000 die as a result of a London smog so thick that men with lanterns lead city buses along the streets. A New York smog in 1953 kills 250. In the fall of 1954, heavy smog shuts down schools and industry in L.A. for most of October.)

By 1960, New York's industrial core is eroding. The port leaves for New Jersey, and city inhabitants follow; for the first time since residents fled town during the Revolution, the New York population declines. The metropolitan area is the great force now, like the severely urbanized region it anchors, which sociologists call Megalopolis, or sometimes Boswash. One in four Americans lives there. November 1965, and the northeastern power grid goes down from Canada to Brooklyn, stranding more than a million New Yorkers in subways and elevators. Splendid in adversity, obnoxious when safe, Gothamites cope with ingenuity, and looting is surprisingly light. The brilliant full moon, police announce, probably saved New York from chaos. For the first time in three hundred years, an untrammeled night sky appears above the city.

But the early sixties also teach ordinary New Yorkers that they can, after all, take a hand in how the city looks, and lives.

Leaf and Stone

An unlikely coalition of Greenwich Village residents, led by the urban critic Jane Jacobs, defeats a superhighway that would have destroyed Manhattan's still-charming downtown. Other civic groups fight off a garbage incinerator at the Brooklyn Navy Yard and a plan to dam the Delaware, the region's last wild river. The 1963 razing of midtown's neoclassical marvel Penn Station catalyzes a historic-preservation movement as surely as the publication of *Silent Spring* drives environmentalists everywhere (even in New York) to organized outcry. Another coalition of commuters and suburbanites defies the progress-first mantra of regional planning authorities to block a fourth New York airport, intended for ten thousand wetland acres in northern New Jersey, the area known today as the Great Swamp National Wildlife Refuge. For the first time in Greater New York history, citizen groups and public-interest forces add a few crucial verbs to the urban vocabulary of built and natural environments alike: *preserve, conserve, rehabilitate, restore.*

City people who like nature know that it is dearest when scarce. Nearly fifty small-animal veterinarians practice in Manhattan, tending to the wolf in the foyer and the tiger in the house. The urban birdwatcher who does morning yoga on her apartment rooftop will always remember glancing up from the crane position to see a line of real cranes, flying along the Hudson. In the blocks near the Union Square Greenmarket, three days a week, you can see New Yorkers staggering home with bushels of farm-grown Ida Reds, flats of daffodils, or six-foot rhododendrons. Corner groceries in Greenwich Village charge ninety-five dollars for a Christmas tree and fifteen dollars for a Halloween pumpkin, in season, and nobody blinks. Staccato queries from the five boroughs fill on-line gardening chat rooms: *How do I make wisteria twine around a fire escape by next week? Who has ideas for preventing window-box theft? What's eating the tomatoes on my balcony? I live on the twenty-eighth floor, for God's sake.*

Urbanites invading the 'burbs, where container gardening is suddenly optional, can find Arcadia troubling. In the suburbs, *nothing* is contained; city transplants wince at the sight of a hawk perched on a streetlight, eating a snake, and flinch from the moths that bump so loudly along the window screens after dark. The standard urban suggestions for dealing with the natural—stomp it, run from it, admire it from a safe distance—do not suit a middle landscape. Garden-center owners and county agents keep lists: the stockbroker who buys fresh sweet corn but stares helplessly at the enfolding husks ("Don't they have a zipper or something?"); the agitated caller to the state ag-department hotline who wants a specialist *immediately* because his evergreens have big, ugly tumors ("Sir, out here, we call those pine cones"). New Yorkers have a lot in common with their houseplants: we humans share 30 percent of our genes with yeast, 80 percent with chickens, and 99 percent with chimps. But break the news gently, in the low zip codes.

Some scholars trace the alienation of Americans from nature to the antebellum shift from a wood culture to a fossil-fuels economy of coal and petroleum, or cite as an emotional point of no return the late nineteenth century's slaughter-orgies of native bison and passenger pigeon. Others blame the Nature Company and The Weather Channel, for turning nature into a marketing opportunity. Still others—biologists, usually, like Edward O. Wilson—argue for the concept of biophilia. Humans evolved as part of nature, they say, and still need it so badly that to live divorced from Earth-knowledge makes us crazy, or mean, or both. Biohype, other commentators snap. More Americans birdwatch and go to zoos than attend pro sports—or attend college. The city is the best means yet to free us from nature's enslavement. Anyone who grew up on a farm, or has tried to clear a single suburban acre, will attest that living close to the earth is no Petit Trianon. Yet urban reactions to nature still range from hate and fear through indifference and uncritical adoration, with trust the most uncommon reaction of all; city types have distrusted nature ever since a hungry eagle mistook Aeschylus' bald Athenian head for a rock and dropped a turtle on it, efficiently cracking the shell of its prey, but killing the playwright. In contemporary urban discourse, depending on who's talking, the nonhuman is to be avoided, imitated, domesticated, exterminated, improved upon, commodified, or left for children to enjoy—nature being a phase you grow out of, like Nintendo, or Barbies. The range of response has rarely been wider. But most of it falls on one side or the other of what Aldo Leopold called the A-B cleavage. Leopold, the author of *A Sand County Almanac* and inventor of the land ethic, learned nature-study within the New York orbit, first at Lawrenceville, then at Yale. A lifetime among forestry and game managers made him realize that even among land professionals, Group A invariably sees land as soil, or real estate, and badly wants to make it produce something, whether crops or cash. Group B perceives the land as a biota, a community; worries about watersheds and wildlife; and wants us to live more lightly upon it.

In this vehement city, hardly anyone opts for C ("nature is

important and nice, if you like that sort of thing"). Some New Yorkers lovingly carry buckets of compost home on the F train, then spend all weekend blending it into the recalcitrant Brooklyn clay with a kitchen fork, like egg whites for soufflé. Others force opossums into metal garbage cans during a July heatwave and let them broil alive. Still others go in for workaday biophilias, like the four Bronx high school boys I watched swagger toward Pelham Park in full thug array: bandanas, gold tooth caps, and impressively baggy pants. Baggy with peanuts, as it turned out; a covey of gray squirrels ran joyfully to them, sat on their shoes, and were gently fed. Other New Yorkers might make even Darwin stare. I was in a cab one November day, coming down Broadway from Columbia to Penn Station, thinking mostly about catching the 2:45, listening with half an ear to the driver's autobiography (civil engineering degree from Calcutta, three unsatisfactory children, New York politics an abomination) when we stopped at a light in the West Sixties, and Mr. Patel's monologue stopped too. "Do you see?" he whispered. Two men on foot were darting through the slow traffic. One was bareheaded, panting, wearing a torn jeans jacket; he vaulted the low stone wall by Central Park and vanished into the leafless underbrush. The other man, sleek and unhurried, wore a chic leather overcoat and a slight smile; in his hand we saw a gun barrel's blue-gray gleam. He looked zestful and pleasantly detached, like a cat tormenting a vole. "Oh, my beauty," said the driver, "this is *not good*." He jumped the light, and the cab fled down Broadway, both of us sitting low, neither of us looking back.

The normally fierce local media make room for nature now and then: the annual feature on circus elephants parading through the Queens Midtown Tunnel to perform at Madison Square Garden, the ritual arrival of the seven-ton Rockefeller Center Christmas tree and its five miles of lights. Hook-and-bullet shows do well in the sports-mad outer boroughs. And news directors all over the metro area endorse a few distinctive categories of nature coverage: harrowing tales of kidnapped parrots, dogs rescued from subway tracks, or cats plucked from skyscraper ledges; reports on nature as a health danger (from record ozone levels to the nine-foot tiger sharks off Coney Island); and the eco-porn of nature-as-enemy shows, whose vivid footage of tornadoes and killer bees makes city children sent off to the country by the Fresh Air Fund very, very anxious.

The New Yorker/nature zone of interaction that most horrifies out-of-towners (visiting parents, especially) is often the first-apartment kitchen: flick on light, look tactfully at the ceiling while the roaches scramble under the baseboards, invite company in. New York cockroaches also like to nest in the cozy innards of office photocopiers, which is why some Manhattan corporations employ roach-eating office geckos. But locals and visitors can be charmed by other manifestations of city nature, some fantastical, some not, like the stainless-steel gargoyles of the Chrysler Building, or the fine stone lions that guard the New York Public Library on Fifth Avenue, named Patience and Fortitude by Mayor Fiorello La Guardia, since these were the virtues he felt New Yorkers most needed to survive the Depression.

Contemporary New Yorkers with little funding but much fortitude have created nearly a thousand school and community gardens in vacant lots, some sketchy, others verging on landscape art. The city keeps trying to bulldoze the improvised green spaces, or auction them off, claiming the acreage is needed for low-income housing. Low-income citizens keep chaining themselves to the apple trees and basil pots, insisting they need gardens too. (During one lot auction, protestors bought ten thousand crickets over the Internet, smuggled them into a police-headquarters meeting in briefcases, and released them in protest. Nearly everyone, including the police, began to scream and stand on chairs. Most of the crickets escaped; most of the protestors were arrested; the auction went ahead as planned, netting the city $19 million, Manhattan real estate prices being what they are.)

Some city manifestations seem positively miragelike, such as the daring kayakers of the Bronx, or the owl-shaped decoy swinging from a Beaux Arts cornice at Madison and Seventy-second, one of the world's most civilized corners, except for its militant pigeons. Others should be mirages, but are not, notably the whole fresh foot-long cow tongues found nailed to an oak tree in the Bronx, with padlocks dangling from each tip ("It appears that someone is encouraging someone else to be silent," observed Parks Commissioner Henry Stern, in a marvel of understatement). Central Park is the headquarters for power birders and extreme birders. In Chinatown, everyone knows where the birds will be: each evening, immigrants from south China carry their songbirds to the community gardens and hang the cages on trees so all can hear, as on a Sung scroll.

New York has a number of working animals still: bookstore cats and restaurant cats, pit bulls and Santeria chickens. Remnant sightings from the age of the horse persist too. Police horses and Central Park carriage horses are stabled on the far West Side, and a number of privately owned riding horses live in the Park Avenue Armory. One misty November morning, I even discovered a troop of cavalry reenactors tying their reins to the iron railings of Madison Square Park at Fifth and Twenty-sixth, preparing for a Veterans Day parade. The sabers and saddle flasks shining in the fog, the immaculate flanks of roan, chestnut and dapple-gray, seemed a moment of time-slip back to the winter of 1875, when George Custer dreamed of a vice-presidential nomination in his midtown hotel, and everyone's music-hall favorites were Captain Jenks of the Horse Marines and the dangerous Mrs. Jenks ("I am Mrs. Jenks of Madison Square/I wear fine clothes and I curl my hair/The Captain went on a regular tear/And they kicked him out of the Army!").

New York City is still part of heavily agricultural New York State, at least according to its land-grant university Cornell, which co-sponsors a 4-H project in the South Bronx to raise and market tank-grown catfish and hydroponic celery. A Harlem cheese-making outpost is to follow. An all-city agricultural product is honey, gleaned from some two dozen rooftop and backyard hives in Brooklyn, Manhattan, and the Bronx. Beekeeping is illegal in New York, owing to the dangerous wild animals involved. But urban honey is sweet and smooth, say connoisseurs; the bees forage for pollen in the community gardens, among the sidewalk flower tubs of a hundred Korean corner groceries, and in Central Park. New York City honey is also exceptionally pure. No intensive farming nearby means fewer heavy-duty pesticides. Some New York bees even commute between the worlds of city nature and city culture: forty thousand were recently released in SoHo as part of an organic art installation, and swarmed dramatically in the streets until residents called the police. The artist explained that they would come home by nightfall, a triumph of conceptual art. The bees did so, keeping perfect union hours, and everyone was content, the rarest of Manhattan outcomes.

One spring afternoon, I walked down Washington Place, across Sixth Avenue, and over to Bank Street to visit a duck that had settled in Greenwich Village. The duck was the biggest attraction for blocks around; whole Village neighborhoods seemed to be wandering by, to watch and worry and marvel. Perfect strangers discussed its habits and its color scheme, saved bagel crumbs for it, called friends on their cell phones about it, and trailed it on its waddling urban rounds, though at a respectful distance. New York has plenty of famous faces, but very few downtown mallards. Most people simply stood quietly and watched the duck watch them, basking in its tonic wildness, looking as though they had received an infusion of vitamins, or happiness, or both. I thought again of biophilia's usual definition: "the innately emotional affiliation of human beings to other living organisms."

"We can never have enough of nature," wrote Henry David Thoreau, who lived in Manhattan and on Staten Island before heading home for a ground-truthing sabbatical at Walden Pond, ". . . in wildness is the preservation of the world." In his exurban second-growth forest, Thoreau listened both to thrush music in the glade and to the daily thunder of the 5:30 local. His Walden Pond cabin stood less than two miles from downtown Concord, but a few hundred yards from the main Boston-Fitchburg train line. Thoreau's famous last words ("Moose . . . Indian") evoke the lost America whose sweet wind haunted hard men all their lives, but the last entry in his journal carefully, lovingly, joins the built and natural worlds, describing how rain and wind write deeply on the gravel of a railroad causeway. Like any thinking New Yorker, he understood that true wilderness can never come back, but he also saw that wildness remains the marrow of civilization. We need it for our tap water, our midtown air, our restaurant dinners. We may need it even more as something unknowable, pressing day and night at the margins of the sanitized life, preceding and sustaining us, outwitting, outlasting.

When I was eleven, I became a licensed game farm. It was my mother's idea, really; she ran a medical library for the state of Wisconsin, housed one corridor away from an animal research lab, and when I visited her at work I would slip down the hall whenever I could, to console the inmates. The sheep minded their predicament least. I often knelt by their pen to scratch their dense, dingy wool, watch the vertical pupils of their goldenrod eyes, and stare at the tangled caps of electrode wire— red, orange, and green—that sprang from their shaven skulls and ran to the big telemetry boards behind their pen. Sheep EEGs are nearly flat. They are not great thinkers. The dozen barn cats hunched in the upper cages thought too much: they *knew* where they were going to end up—on the shelves of cat brains in the next room, afloat in formaldehyde the color of tobacco smoke, labeled "Polydactyl Feline, Frontal Lobe 601A" or "Polydactyl Feline, Frontal Lobe 601B." Polydactyl Feline 601C was a limber tortoiseshell that broke out of every cage the center possessed; eventually we took her home, along with a squirming baby raccoon destined for the same set of neurophysiology experiments: two pounds of silky gray fur, with eager, searching handlike paws and round bright black eyes set off by the bandit's mask of his kind.

The cat—Cee—proved to have perfect manners, but no small talk. Shadow—Shad—was an insomniac, and a yakker. At first we thought he would live happily in the basement by night, but instead he would bound to the top step and trill furiously, beating at the door. I became fluent at translating raccoon comments, which are mostly in the imperative: "Look what I found"; "Out of the way or I'll bite you"; "Give me *all* your lunch"; and, sometimes, late at night, "Come and scratch me, I'm feeling insecure." After that particular warbling call, a small agitated paw would slide out from under the closed basement door, patting and searching the hardwood floor. I would touch one finger to the prehensile palm and he would grip it hard, burble and churr for a bit, then fall asleep, still holding on.

Shad soon moved upstairs to sleep in my sock drawer (his idea), and then denned atop my canopy bed, climbing the posts like a midshipman in rigging and tumbling about. Raccoons are both adventurous and social: he liked to sit on my shoulders and cling to my head during fast bike rides, gripping my ponytail for balance. He liked baths too, and would rush uninvited to the tub and scramble up, over, and in—*whee!*—which houseguests found unnerving. In time, Shad grew to nearly forty pounds before he returned to the woods for his own wild nights, though he never forgot the way to our refrigerator, which he explored like a spelunker, tossing bottles and bags over his shoulder in fine abandon until he located a bunch of grapes or a chocolate cookie.

Raccoons are natural safecrackers and learn the world

largely by touch, looking thoughtfully into the middle distance as they pop open promising jam jars, unwind whole packages of rickrack, or undo essential furniture screws. Shad could disassemble a double box of Christmas ornaments in a night, shiny globes heaped here, silver hooks laid out there, and a pile of gold caps in between, never making a mistake in category, and never breaking one. He liked classical music on TV, Bartók especially, but hated commercials, and would climb atop the set, seize the channel dial with both paws, and click through the stations, hunting for a nature documentary, or at least a sitcom. If remotes had been around then, he would have adored them.

But even more than watching television, he liked to watch my dreams. Many nights I would fall into sleep with a full-grown raccoon chirring quietly on my pillow, and wake hours later to feel cool paw pads resting lightly on my closed lids, tracking each eyeball flicker with patient interest. The animal touch in the moonlight was as impersonal as a doctor's, delicate, curious, relentless, infinitely other.

Three

Day and Night

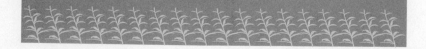

The Old Neighborhood

When I was in grade school, I played every day in the ruins of a lost city. A lost suburb, really; in 1911, a consortium of developers decided that what Madison, Wisconsin, really needed was a nine-hundred-acre Venetian fantasy at the edge of town, with conveniences modern and Renaissance—a chain of lagoons, a shaded mall, a shopping center. They sold nearly a hundred lots, laid out concrete streets and sidewalks, installed the water and phone lines, and plotted an ambitious causeway across a marsh where Winnebago hunting camps had stood just a dozen years before. The first houses rose on schedule. But by 1920, the imposing boulevard was still a single-lane road—its wetland footings kept sinking, expensively—and by 1922 the project was a morass of defaulted loans, failed mortgage bonds, and jail sentences. Frost cracked the paved streets; grass and weeds grew in the new foundations. Half-dredged lagoons became drainage ditches, full of wild blackberry and fallen trees. The bird and panther mounds nearby, cleared as Indian-lore curiosities, vanished once more, under second-growth forest. The local farmers went back to farming, in desultory Depression fashion; the area's soil was nearly worn out, and nearby Lake Wingra was full of silt and duckweed.

But all through the 1930s, another consortium—of townspeople and university professors—quietly bought twelve hundred acres of land in and around the lost city. They wanted to make an arboretum, but a wild one, a restored wilderness in the middle of a metropolis, to reflect in perfect miniature the oak-hickory forest and tallgrass meadows encountered by its first white settlers a hundred years before. A Wisconsin professor of game management named Aldo Leopold was especially adamant about learning to read the landscape you live in. If we fail to recover our natural past, he said, there will be no future. "We have realized we have introduced unintentional and unneccessary changes which threaten to undermine the future capacity of the environment to support our civilization," he warned in 1938, at the arboretum's dedication. When a reporter asked one of the ecologists how long it would take to restore this stretch of second-rate farmland and dead suburb to the original mix of lake and prairie, the scientist replied, "Roughly . . . a thousand years."

By the mid-1960s, a zoning quirk had allowed a dozen new houses (ours included) to be built at the edge of the vanished settlement; otherwise, more development never touched it. But the lure of forested ruins three miles from downtown meant that hikers often turned up in our driveway on sunny weekends, asking the way to the Lost City. I would lean out from my tree house and give directions with the brisk impatience of a New Yorker asked to point out the Empire State Building: turn right at the foot of the hill to find the old foundations and cellar holes, turn left to walk the crumbling avenue. In four or five hours, I knew, they would be back, covered in burrs, agitated, sweaty, pleading to call a cab back to town. Modern ruins made them uneasy: too recent, too real.

When I was in grade school, my father and I drove every day along the remains of the old boulevard in our blue Ford station wagon, the one with the fins, and the seats like park benches. When I was in high school, we had to go around by the lake instead, because the honeysuckle and bittersweet were moving in, shrinking the last street to a bike path. By the time I finished college and went east, the suppressed springs were rising, making ponds in the road and deepening the ditches on either side. A quarter-century later, I walked down the hill and looked for the road through the woods again, but could barely find it. The boulevard is a deer trail now, though if you kneel to part the weeds, the broken concrete is still there, under the leaf mold. Beside the grandest of the Venetian canals, swampy with cow parsley and bog iris, a gray fox trotted toward the eight-lane highway at the arboretum's edge. You can hear the roar of traffic all the time in the lost city now; like Ann Arbor, like Boulder, like Austin, Madison has doubled and tripled its population, the gently eccentric college town overwhelmed by office parks and fitness centers: a fragmented habitat, at least for me. The forest that ate a suburb has itself been made an island environment by exurban sprawl. Sightseers still come by the vanload, though, looking for the best road to the local urban legend, the lost city in the woods. But there is no road through the woods.

As Alexandros Washburn and Marijke Smits drive the industrial backroads of the New Jersey Meadowlands, one studies the map and the other the terrain. Then they trade. Neither watches the road much, which makes their progress meandering and slow. Fortunately, traffic in rural Secaucus is thin, and stoplights few, here in muskrat and warehouse country. They are looking for a legendary landfill, knowing only that if they cross the Northeast Corridor rail tracks they have gone too far. Smits, in her mid-twenties, slender, calm, and blond, is in charge of history and archaeology for the Penn Station Redevelopment Corporation, a New York state agency; Washburn, in his mid-thirties, brown-haired and energetic, is the corporation president. Both are easy in the presence of the past, having grown up around historians and archaeologists, archives and digs. Neither really expects to find two vast column drums of rosy granite beside a fire hydrant in the parking lot of a North Jersey trucking company. "Oh, my God," says Washburn, staring. "It's either Stonehenge—or Penn Station."

An architect by training, Alex Washburn used to be public works adviser to Daniel Patrick Moynihan, the former senior United States Senator from New York. A few years ago, Moynihan told him: Here's your new job: get a new Penn Station built. And, by the way, find the old one too. Make it rise again from the Meadowlands.

Knowing only that the remains of Manhattan's original Pennsylvania Station had been unceremoniously dumped in the New Jersey marshlands, Washburn and Smits and assorted volunteers have, in their off hours, been searching ever since, digging, mapping, hoping, probing the Secaucus backlands for broken balustrades and Ionic capitals, columns and caryatids. They've learned to decipher faded aerial photos from Army Corps of Engineers archives; to wear hip waders in their search (*not* business suits); to beware of snapping turtles; to recon-

struct the tale of a misplaced American icon. They'd like to res-
urrect this urban Titanic. They have to find it first. "We want to
make the mute stones speak," Washburn explains, "but unfortu-
nately there's no budget line in the Penn Station redevelopment
plan for 'archaeological treasure.' "

The Jersey Meadowlands are thirty-two square miles of
remnant cedar forest, rusting auto bodies, perpetually burning
garbage dumps, and cattail bog. Parts of the great swamp have
been filled in for office parks and malls and sports arenas, and
other sections converted to landfill. Farther north, in Hackensack, are the really big fill sites—the Meadowlands garbage
mountains, where methane miners recover enough gas each
year to supply two large townships and a school system. But
the middle, or Secaucus, reach, just as wild, just as polluted, is
where millions of tons of New York architectural and construction fill ended up, whole neighborhoods reduced to rubble.
Its blackwater inlets are crisscrossed by train tracks on em-
bankments and expressways on stilts; beyond the Weehawken
Heights at the eastern swamp edge, where Aaron Burr once du-
eled Alexander Hamilton, you can see the Manhattan skyline.
On a golden afternoon in early October, Marijke Smits leads a
group of searchers deep into the high grasses and sumac behind
the National Retail Systems trucking lot and its parked fleet of
eighteen-wheel tractor-trailers. Pheasants and warblers scatter
overhead. Only a glimpse of the World Trade Center towers
above the willows, plus the Amtrak trains pounding along the
nearby embankment, hint that we are just six miles from Times
Square.

"Hey, Marijke! Here's Penn Station!" says a young digger,
jumping into a drainage ditch and pushing back a cloud of

Queen Anne's lace. He's almost right: half-buried amid broken brick and concrete and stained PVC pipe is an eight-foot slab of the station's characteristic pink granite, mortared on one side, cleanly cut on the other. Among the phragmites and milkweed nearby lie scattered squares of white tile and glass block. "Those could be from the bathrooms on Penn Station's old commuter level," says a pleased Smits, "but this plinth is definitely from the building itself. A hunk of size." We crouch, and gaze, and touch the sun-warmed stone.

The Gilded Age liked its construction projects heroic—the Brooklyn Bridge, the Panama Canal—and the creation of the New York City terminus of the Pennsylvania Railroad did not disappoint. Five hundred buildings in the Manhattan slum neighborhood Hell's Kitchen were razed to make room for a nine-acre train station whose concourse was longer than the nave of Saint Peter's in Rome, whose waiting room was a deliberate cross between the Baths of Caracalla and the Basilica of Constantine. Erecting Penn Station took four years (1906–10) and consumed nearly thirty thousand tons of steel, and more than six hundred granite pillars. Twenty-eight Beaux Arts eagles, plus four heroic pairs of classical maidens—each beautifully detailed set representing Day and Night—guarded the station's four colonnaded façades.

When railroad president Alexander Cassatt (brother of painter Mary Cassatt) suggested some practical touches—adding a hotel, sticking to a budget—architect Charles McKim of the gilt-edged firm McKim, Mead, and White was appalled. New York, he declared, must have a portal as imposing as the city, and as solid, "a thoroughly and distinctly monumental gateway." Details mattered deeply, and provenance too: Penn Station's exterior was a rosy granite quarried in Massachusetts, but the honey-colored travertine for the lower walls within was proudly ordered from the same Tivoli quarries that supplied the builders of Rome's Colosseum. Modern competitors had to be outdone as well. Paris and London boasted exhibition halls and rail sheds trellised with iron and skylights like vast gazebos, so Penn Station designers added a 138-foot vault to their open concourse, then pierced it with acres of glass ribbed in steel. Day and night, Pennsy passengers moved toward their trains through great shafts of sun- or moonlight. Unlike its merrier rival Grand Central, fifteen blocks away, the completed Penn Station was complex, ambiguous, and shadowy; easy to get lost in, and hard to love. But more than any other New York public space it seemed always "murmurous," as novelist Thomas Wolfe observed, "with the immense and distant sound of time. Few buildings are vast enough to hold the sound of time, and . . . there was a superb fitness in the fact that the one which held it better than all the others should be a railroad station."

Neither architect nor patron lived to see the station's opening. Neither imagined their sumptous transport temple could be sidetracked by history. But throughout the Depression, hundreds of homeless slept in Penn Station each night; after the war, with its rush of troop trains and late-night partings, the great terminal turned steadily quieter, dirtier, scarier. City soot dimmed the pink walls, and a jukebox array of decorative elements crept in, from turntable car displays to a hideous plastic clamshell suspended over the ticket booths. Nothing helped. When developers sought to replace the urban dinosaur with a smaller, trendier complex, many commuters shrugged; many New Yorkers cheered. In October 1963, demolition commenced, and regrets as well. "Until the first blows fell," wrote a *New York Times* editorialist, "no one was convinced that Penn Station really would be demolished or that New York would permit this modern act of vandalism. . . . Any city gets what it admires, will pay for, and ultimately deserves. We want and deserve tin-horn architecture in a tin-horn culture. And we will probably be judged not by the monuments we build but by those we have destroyed."

By late 1966, New Yorkers looked at the blocks between Seventh and Eighth Avenues and Thirty-first and Thirty-third Streets and saw, at the edge of the garment district, a Roman ruin. When only the station's decapitated foundation was left, a wrecking company carted Penn Station's remains to a dump site in the Meadowlands. In 1968, a *New York Times* photographer ventured into the Secaucus marshes and returned with a wrenching shot of a Penn Station figure of Day, toppled and broken in an architectural killing field of neoclassical rubble beside the Pennsy tracks. A few years later, no one remembered precisely where the old Penn Station lay. Other buildings, other neighborhoods, had been dropped on top of it: nineteenth-century tenements, twentieth-century garages and candy stores. No one kept records of what fell to earth where, or in what order. And over the decades, the landfill sites were repeatedly bulldozed, shifting landscape contours, blurring memory, jumbling time.

But for architectural preservationists of the seventies, the eighties, and the nineties, the *idea* of lost Penn Station, that martyred monument, proved exceptionally powerful, and useful too. Penn Station's destruction accelerated the creation of the New York City Landmarks Preservation Commission in 1965, and helped inspire the founding of the National Register of Historic Places. Yet in the fall of 1963, when the president of the failing Pennsylvania Railroad plaintively inquired, "Does it make any sense to preserve a building merely as a monument?" all concerned (even the polite black-armbanded picketers at the demolition site) knew the answer, or believed they did. In the march of modernity and progress through midtown Manhattan, there was simply no place for a classical tepidarium, however noble it made you feel on the way to the 5:32.

For the next forty years, to get to the second Penn Station, you went to Seventh Avenue, where Macy's faces Thirty-fourth Street, and turned south to find the Penn Plaza/Madison Square Garden complex, a vintage sixties smoked-glass office slab attached to a circular sports and entertainment center of stained beige concrete, in whose basement is still the world's busiest railroad terminal, forced completely underground but carrying more rail traffic than anyone dreamed possible in 1963. By 2000, Penn Station II had half a million users every day; during rush hour, one thousand people every ninety seconds braved its dank, low-ceilinged maze. ("Then, one entered the city like a god," mourned Yale architectural critic Vincent Scully, remembering the original terminal. "Now one scuttles in like a rat.")

But when Penn Station moves across Eighth Avenue to the rehabbed General Post Office building (designed by McKim, Mead, and White as a massive companion to Cassatt's great station), this third incarnation will be decorated with spolia from the ruins of the first. Marijke Smits has spent years tracking bits of the lost Penn Station. Candelabra from its main waiting room were discovered in storage at the Cathedral of Saint John the Divine. An original chandelier was spotted in Houston. A stone eagle was found nesting in an apartment on Manhattan's West Side. "I *dream* about Penn Station, all the time," says Smits. "Claustrophobic dreams, of a place I never saw. It's probably the photos of the building's last days, which are heartbreaking."

Strangers, mostly elderly, call her all the time, offering pictures, relics, memories. One couple saved a half dozen brass and leather stools from the station coffee shop, snatching them from the rubble, lugging them home in a Checker Cab. Others stashed bits of salvage in attic or yard for nearly four decades, like the New Jersey newspaperman who drove into the Meadowlands to load the family Ford with carved-stone fragments. A pair of perfect granite balusters have sat beside his suburban front porch for thirty years, pedestals for flower pots. These too will return. The larger the pieces, the more elusive their fates. One of Penn Station's Doric columns was hauled to upstate New York to adorn a small college that was never built. Today it stands alone in a hilltop birch grove, smeared with graffiti. Other columns may still be buried in the Meadowlands. The station's fourteen stone eagles were originally carted to a parking lot off West Thirty-first Street, in case someone wanted them. Philadelphia has four. One went to Canada for Expo '67, and was briefly held hostage by Montreal's eagle-loving mayor. Another traveled to Hicksville, New York, at the request of the local high school classics teacher. (Students greeted its arrival with flaming torches, the Pledge of Allegiance recited in Latin, and a special serenade from band members dressed in togas.)

For Washburn and Smits, the recovery project's grail is a missing pair of allegorical figures: a ten-ton maiden representing Day—crowned in bayberry, upraised face framed by carved sunflowers—and her companion, Night, a young woman with averted face who cradles a sheaf of poppies. Four Day and four Night figures guarded the original Penn Station. One pair became the centerpiece of the Eagle Scout Tribute Fountain in Kansas City (and they're not coming back, officials there say; finders keepers). Another pair, rescued from the Meadowlands mud, was taken to a park in northern New Jersey, and will be displayed in Newark. A third Day-Night pair has long been separated: a lone Night figure lives in the sculpture garden at the Brooklyn Museum of Art, and in mid-1998 a recycling company in the Bronx informed Alex Washburn that a badly damaged Day had been sitting in its yard for years.

Which leaves a final pair missing in action. Although their principal mandate is to catalog finds and try for donations, Washburn and Smits keep searching the marshes. They would like to find an eagle, or a scrolled column capital; they would *love* to find the lost Day and Night. Some older New Jersey Transit trainmen have told Marijke Smits that after a brush or marsh fire, you can still see great pieces of marble in the reed beds near the tracks. Landfill owners, sensing fame, have begun boasting that *their* lots hold mysterious classical fragments *too*. For now, Smits and Washburn are concentrating on the truck lot near the Secaucus train tunnel, where the former Pennsy tracks, still heavily used, run under the Hudson River to midtown Manhattan. On every possible weekend, one or both board the New York Waterways ferry and churn across the Hudson to Weehawken, armed with aged photos of the Meadowlands. Aided by urban archaeology irregulars with trucks and shovels and a taste for ruins, these impromptu expeditions have been roaming the swamps to find Penn Station's bones, pushing warily through seven-foot stands of phragmites, probing the polluted ponds, scrambling up willows to look for landmarks thirty years gone, and occasionally stumbling on the sunflower meadows that flourish even in the Meadowlands, the most polluted urban wilderness in Greater New York. When the search team found an especially beautiful hidden patch of sunflowers one summer day, they took it as a sign ("We were all punchy," admits Marijke Smits) and gathered armfuls in honor of their quest for Day and Night. Even finance majors and urban planners, suitably motivated, will wave sheaves of blossom among the reeds to appease the swamp gods, and perhaps persuade a lost Day statue to surface, foot-wide marble sunflowers gloriously intact.

What they got instead was Ron LaBarca of Matawan, New Jersey. LaBarca, head of the imaging firm U.S. Radar, is a history buff who saw a local-newspaper piece about the search for Penn Station and asked Smits if she would like to borrow his ground-penetrating radar, a technology used by utility companies to find abandoned power lines, by law enforcement to find drug caches and skeletons—and by archaeologists to locate difficult sites. Sitting in LaBarca's van one fall day, waiting for Marijke to finish a tricky map comparison, I asked why he had made the offer. "Why not?" he said, surprised. "The past isn't past. It's all there. The ground doesn't lie. You just have to be persistent. Also a little crazed."

Two of his largest radar units (which look like oversized yellow lawn mowers with computer screens fitted to the handlebars) have been imported for intensive scanning of the truck lot nearest the tracks. LaBarca and an assistant move slowly across the cracked and muddy search ground, veering now and then to miss puddles, potholes, and stray axles, letting the radar pierce the ground like a knife edge, three, four, six feet deep. The green lines of the readout form an image of the urban wreckage beneath the postmodern asphalt.

"Complex rubble," says LaBarca, intrigued. "Weird stuff." He turns the machine once more, plowing a neat, invisible furrow across the lot.

"Ron—try one and a half meters."

LaBarca looks at the changing radar signature, a flurry of parabolas, and does a double take.

"*Hel*-lo. That's a column. Lots of columns. I think probably statues too. Good sleuth work. Hey, Marijke!"

Smits looks up from her rolls of yellowed maps. "The mother lode?"

LaBarca grins. Smits pumps the air, then runs to join him. They bend tenderly over the corroded asphalt, too happy to talk much, marking each potential find with arrows and scribbles in colored chalk, a basis for an excavation grid, and a guide for the vacuum trucks that will strip away the layers of fill and the flatbed trucks that may someday carry the finds back across the river, across the years, to Thirty-third Street once more. LaBarca pirouettes his machine to check the edges of the site, and on the monitor the transmissions sharpen and blur and sharpen, the past surfacing into the present like a breaching whale.

If some of the original Penn Station can be recalled to midtown Manhattan, why not restore some of the city's original nature, the ultimate environmental reparation? New York, after all, specializes in creative destruction: building up, tearing down, moving around, rebuilding. Why *not* steam-clean the harbor, reseed the oysters, replace invasive phragmites with native salt grass, revamp the skyline lights to let the songbirds pass?

Environmental historians, wildlife biologists, politicians, and urban experts all begin to hyperventilate at the prospect, for different reasons. The arguments pile up, the interpretations turn ever more fluid and contrary, always with a subtext of real uncertainty and doubt: what *is* wild, these days? Maybe we should look for new definitions of wildness between the cracks of a Brooklyn sidewalk, in a neighbor's affection for plastic lawn flamingos, in a swamp filled with classical columns, in our own turbulent bloodstreams. Defining *natural* is harder still, since even designated North American wildernesses are very large parks in disguise, with rangers, permits, and posted trails; only a handful of Alaska mountains and Nevada alkali plateaus remain officially unmapped. Ought we be calling these few untouched environments "first nature" and everything else "second nature," as the British cultural critic Raymond Williams proposed? Or, instead of the long-running either-or standoff of front lawn versus wilderness, would it be more grown-up to make the garden our model instead?

No, saving scenic grandeur is fine, say some economists—but let the market solve pollution and efficient-energy problems, since the key to keeping wide open spaces wide and open is to keep people urban, and to leave more space for puma. The city is efficient, productive, and concentrated, and therefore ecological. It's the suburbs that are killing us. Not at all, say suburban advocates; the city is a parasite, intensely consuming and producing waste, with an environmental footprint that can be hundreds of miles wide. New York alone needs twenty thousand tons of food hauled in daily by truck, train, ship, and plane; its hungers are global.

But New York's newly wild urban nights also mark a real change in city-country relations, the first in many centuries. More and more scholars now suggest that even a megacity is part of a larger land-use story, in which cities are as vulnerable to nature and fortune as any other life-form; some endure, some thrive, some shrink. Some vanish. Other critics are repelled by talk of the lifespan of cities, or the decay and regeneration of suburbs. Cities are artifacts, they insist, designed to abstract nature, at a profit, over a distance, turning cows into hamburger and redwoods into plywood. Yet if you lived and worked with skyscrapers and bridges, New York City engineers retort, you would know they really *are* living organisms, which suffer and die if not maintained. Just remember that, like mountains, their timescales are not ours.

Nor are their worries. Faced with forest, desert, prairie, river, humans tend to make a space in the midst of, force a path through, beat back. But the price of dominion still troubles us, if only in poetry, or dreams: the lone and level sands stretching away from the toppled statue; the great globe dissolving into illusion; the white whale, hunted, that turns to hunt us. The biblical text least likely to be quoted by developers remains the prophet Isaiah's vision of the heron in the living room. ("Woe unto them that join house to house, that lay field to field, till there be no place that they may be alone in the midst of the earth!") But the problem of contingency—if we push too hard, what then?—seems to apply in prophecy as well as history. Isaiah suggests one answer, and one winner: "Yet soon they will call, and none shall be there; thorns will come up in the palaces, nettles and brambles in the fortresses; it shall be a habitation of dragons, and a court for owls . . . the wild beasts of the island shall dwell in it, says the Lord of Hosts. . . . I will make it a possession for the cormorant, and a home for the bittern."

On a rainy April afternoon in Manhattan I went to see Alexander Brash, who heads the Urban Park Service, to ask how the sixteenth century is coming along. Brash is an articulate and practical Yale Forestry School graduate whose Fifth Avenue office is equipped with both a dart gun and a net gun, since he gets a lot of calls these days reporting wild turkeys sitting in trees, particularly on Manhattan's West Side. With the blessing of New York City Parks Commissioner Henry Stern, and the help of schoolchildren, area environmental groups, and the city's corps of urban rangers, Brash and his staff are running a restoration effort called Project X, whose goal is to return one animal and one plant species every year to each of the five boroughs.

After a few fizzles, like the heavily hyped release of luna moths, which enraged some biologists and environmentalists to the point of apoplexy—luna pupae overwinter in leaf litter at the base of trees, where soccer players can stomp on them, and rats eat them—the Xers began to practice community politics as well as community ecology, consulting New York's abundance of arcane interest groups, from the American Littoral Society to the Friends of the Fishes. Like other restoration groups (such as the multiagency Harbor Estuary Program, which since

1987 has patiently replanted miles of tough native salt grass, cleaned up bights and beaches, and restored city wetlands), the Project X group has discovered the hard way that low-key reintroductions work best. Decorator species like puma will not be coming back to the city on taxpayer money, tempting though it is to make the local food web fully authentic by releasing wolves in Central Park. Nor will black widow spiders or poison ivy make the renaturalization lists. Species that are native to this place and aesthetically pleasing are the favored Project X candidates, like the spring peepers and frogs recently reintroduced to city ponds and woodlands to let city children hear how a June night sounded when Harlem was farm country, and the South Bronx a forest.

Brash and his staff are trying *not* to repeat the ecological mistakes of Central Park's builders, or of New York's urban-renewal czars. Though geniuses of urban design, Olmsted and Vaux and Robert Moses, zealous for big effects fast, also threw entire ecosystems out of whack, through species isolation or simple neglect (making Central Park the only show in town often left the rest of New York nature undertended and under-funded). In re-creating the New York ecological web, you want common species with strong nerves that will take to mega-city life, given some home comforts, and not scare humans or make conspicuous messes. Imports often don't work: release a Westchester bat in Manhattan and it will be home in one day, thoroughly peeved. Habitat upgrades are an X specialty, from nesting poles for osprey to boxes for bats to the kestrel shelters placed on the Pelham Bay landfill in the Bronx, as a way of encouraging the raptors that hunt among the garbage mounds. The reinstated screech owls of Central Park are doing nicely:

surviving, marking territory, bonding with one another. But the twenty chipmunks released there are either MIA or AWOL; no one knows. Possibly the owls ate them.

Some Project X plants get picked. Others get mowed. But nodding trillium has survived to set seed in the Bronx, and an experimental stand of heart-leaved aster there is doing fine, well away from people, in Seton Falls Park, as pearly everlasting (with some surreptitious mulching) is once more thriving on Staten Island. Skunk cabbage, which once grew all over Manhattan Island, did not take to postmodern life, and the covey of bobwhite quail released in the Bronx may have encountered the local feral cats, though a few of the birds have been spotted alive. Reintroduced toads, crayfish, golden shiners, and largemouth bass are all doing well in Brooklyn, as are ebony jewelwing damselflies in Manhattan and the checkerspot butterfly in Queens. American strawberrybush has been reintroduced in Queens as well, where it helps to stabilize eroding hillsides. (A threatened species, it has not been seen in the city since 1923.) Flying squirrels, which were, historically, in all the bigger city parks, still make a home in Pelham, Inwood, and Prospect, sites that may support larger releases, like spotted turtles, groundhogs, and eastern cottontail. American chestnuts, which used to make up one-third of northern hardwood forests, would be an excellent urban restoration; with the help of the American Chestnut Foundation, Project X has planted two new blight-resistant strains at opposite ends of Central Park, and will wait and see.

Waiting and seeing is a major activity in biodiversity restoration, whether you track the results by ground-truthing or by satellite—or both, as the New York workers are doing. No other

city, no other nation, has tried this kind of systematic public re-
vival of a lost landscape. But all restorations—of wolves in Min-
nesota, of otters in a British river, of ocelots to a Guatemalan
rainforest—must be able to supply a clear answer to three uncomfortable questions: Who are you restoring *for*? And *which*
time period are you trying to recapture? And will your restorations stabilize? Alexander Brash is trying for New York as it was
around 1500, just before the Lenape and the Mohicans started
to noticeably alter the area.

"We're looking to replicate a natural, unfarmed wooded
landscape, with the basic species pool intact. Maybe slightly
grazed, but no burn cycle yet. A New York of tall trees, with the
understory intact, and the wildflowers. Clean bodies of fresh
water, and the soil not full of heavy-duty crud. It's a restoration
not pegged to one moment in time. But yes, it is a vision com-
patible with the city of today, or what the city *could* be." He
shrugs. "Whatever you do is going to change. Maybe—very
likely—the whole environment will never all work together
again. We are only trying to give each species a new chance, especially those wiped out by man's hand." (But we *are* in New
York, another staffer notes. So we're looking for catchy things.)

I walk up Fifth Avenue to the park's nature center, on the
banks of Harlem Meer, to see a Project X–sponsored bat pre-
sentation. Thirty second-graders bounce in their chairs, wild to
see the educational bats, which have just taken a cab from the
NBC studios at Rockefeller Plaza: big brown bats and pallid
bats and silverbacked bats, all survivors of bat-car collisions, or
too-close encounters with paranoid humans wielding tennis
rackets and Louisville Sluggers. Some animals the bat conservation group can rehabilitate and release. Others will spend their

days in a Michigan sanctuary. Quite a few prove to have the right personality for show business, especially the one-pound Egyptian fruit bat (fawn-colored body, sleek cream racing stripe), which has already spent much of the morning perched on Matt Lauer's head during a live broadcast of the *Today* show. Unfazed by the squealing crowd, the bats flex wings, crawl obligingly over a handler's sweater, eat mealworms, and echolocate into a handheld amplifier, a susurration of taps and clicks as the animals' sonar maps the size of the room, the wriggling shapes of the immature humans all around them, and the contours of the East Side skyline beyond the window. "That's the New York *you* don't hear—the echolocation clicks of bats," the handler tells the second-graders, who begin to click back, in the manner of an Egyptian fruit bat with a fan club and a Web site.

Location, location. Sometimes a city's site is so well chosen that although populations wax and wane, the area is never really abandoned, no matter how hard the times: think Paris, Marseilles, Istanbul, Jerusalem. Sometimes settlements disappear because the climate changes, like the thirteenth-century Viking colonies on Greenland, whose farms fell victim to the deepening medieval chill of the Little Ice Age, or the cities of the ancient Middle East, whose fertile countryside was so thoroughly retaken by the desert that whole urban populations had to move hundreds of miles north and west. Observers like Jared Diamond point out that if we define a collapse of society as a local drastic decrease in human population numbers and/or in political, economic, or social complexity, many societies have collapsed. In our time, the list would include Zaire, the former Soviet Union, and the former Yugoslavia; in previous centuries, Angkor Wat, the classic lowland Maya world, and the Roman Empire. Some disappearances are, of course, really slow-motion evolutions: there are plenty of Maya still in Mexico and Belize, though thoroughly disenfranchised, but very few Latin speakers in the Piazza Navona.

Isolated island societies find trouble when population outgrows resources, as on Easter Island, where tree cover was stripped for fuel, which led to topsoil erosion, which led to crop failure and famine, which led to a 75 percent population drop. Mainland societies can die the same way. The Anasazi settlements of the American Southwest—sites we know as Chaco, or Walnut Canyon, or Mesa Verde—were flourishing cities between A.D. 900 and A.D. 1300, with trade links that stretched from Ohio to the Andes. But hubris and climate change seem to have combined to doom them too; once surrounding woodlands were mined for kindling and construction timber, the mass deforestation killed the water supply, which may have left residents unusually vulnerable to invaders from the south, or to religious manias, or to cannibalism as a political terror weapon—or maybe all three; experts are still debating. At Chaco a cityful of people walked away from apartment buildings full of possessions, apparently driven out by the consequences of their own environmental overreach, plus bad luck in the form of a decades-long drought.

Sometimes ecological degradation will push a troubled or weakened society over the edge into chaos and darkness. Sometimes enviro-abuse is one of many contributing factors. The lowland Maya fell prey to conquest and disease, but the archaeological record at their great metropolis Copán strongly suggests they had already stripped their jungle mountainsides of vegetation, in part to burn limestone into lime stucco to create magnificent architecture for a demanding elite, in part to feed a growing city. No roster of temples and pyramids, mathematics and hieroglyphics, courts and concerts, could rescind so open an invitation to flooding and famine and landslide, any more than Mayan rulers could be persuaded not to sponsor soccer teams that played ball with severed enemy heads (or, sometimes, with the heads of last week's losing side).

Human-induced ecological processes, anthropogenic turmoil, self-inflicted disaster: all can translate, eventually, to environmental suicide. Large-scale human-settlement projects usually get into trouble through a very few, very bad habits. We overreach, settling in too fast without thinking ahead about where we will put the parking lots and the nuclear waste. Or else we crowd, undermining our chances for a long-term stay by forcing the land to exceed its carrying capacity. If you try this in an obviously fragile environment, like the Great Plains, historians call it the Too-Much Mistake—too many wells, too much plowing, too much effort put into making Nebraska look like Vermont. But even in the leafy New York exurbs, the effect is, eventually, the same, if you throw in enough duplicate copies of the two-hundred-store mall, the seventy-eight-inch television, the two-hour commute, and the five-thousand-calorie dinner.

The Rorschach of lost cities is still ancient Rome, that busy, confident, achieving world so unlike us in its meddling gods and its slave-based economy and its happy ignorance of decimals, so familiar otherwise. From Ireland to the Black Sea, the Roman way cloned itself repeatedly for three hundred years—marketplace, basilica, temple, stadium, baths. It was a transcontinental, multinational culture of sewers, income taxes, fashion designers, best-sellers, political scandals, gourmet chefs, and pro sports that just . . . disappeared. Unraveling, contemplating, and avoiding a repeat of that primal urban fall has been a major task of Western history and thought for the last fifteen centuries. Theories about how and why Rome went under have occupied whole armies of scholars. Too much lead in the pottery glaze. Too many Senate millionaires. Too many outlanders allowed to buy citizenship. Too many crazies in power positions. Too little attention paid to a rural millennialist cult out of Judea. Too much Saxon violence.

But environmental problems now appear to have played a considerable part in the decline of the ancient world as well. Studies of Arctic ice cores, which let researchers track the presence of heavy metals in the atmosphere, reveal that ancient smelters and open-air furnaces released as much lead at the height of the Roman Empire as did Europe's factories during the Industrial Revolution. When Rome falls, the air clears. Both Greeks and Romans knew all about deforestation, agricultural decline, and urban pollution. "There are mountains in Attica," Plato wrote, "which can now keep nothing but bees, but which were clothed, not so very long ago, with . . . timber suitable for roofing the very largest buildings. . . . The annual supply of rainfall was not lost, as it is at present, through being allowed to flow over the denuded surface to the sea." Tertullian, centuries later, noted, "All places are now accessible . . . cultivated fields have subdued forests; flocks and herds have expelled wild beasts . . . everywhere are houses, and inhabitants, and settled governments, and civilized life. What most frequently meets our view is our teeming population; our wants grow more and more keen, while nature fails in affording us her usual sustenance." The ancient world, historian J. Donald Hughes reminds us, suffered from soil erosion, salinization of drinking water and cropland, wildlife depletion, extractive industries, and industrial toxins, particularly mercury pollution. Population booms, resource depletion, deforestation, urban flooding, even the beginnings of environmental awareness: the Empire's regions knew, but did not act.

A few years ago I visited an archaeological dig in Wiltshire, west of London, in a wooded valley near the river town of Hungerford. The dig was run by Stanford and Indiana Universities, but the bills were largely paid by Alexander Abraham, a Wall Street banker with a passion for ruins. The building being recovered was a grand country villa built in the late third and early fourth centuries A.D., at the height of Roman power in Britain. The local name for the site was Castle Copse, appropriate for a hilltop house now deep in woods.

Like all archaeological expeditions, the Castle Copse dig looks like a construction site, littered with surveying tools, yellow plastic buckets, and mounds of Roman rubble. Sunburned groups of diggers kneel among the sixteen-hundred-year-old foundations, scraping cautiously at the battered stone. A corner of mosaic is visible at one trench edge. "I want it down to *chalk!*" yells the dig master. "Make it *gleam!*"

Castle Copse is a villa with a central courtyard plan, its stone walls three feet thick and three hundred feet long, enclosing complexes of rooms sixty feet across. The property had elegant plunge baths, hot-air heating, a central fountain, and a charming garden terrace. Shopping and theater in Londoninium and Aquae Sulis (London and Bath, to us) would have been a pleasant carriage excursion away. Britannia was not at all fashionable; Roman troops had to be paid triple to invade it, and for a long time it remained a hardship posting, a sunless resource colony efficiently mined for grain, tin, wood, silver, and slaves. But over four centuries of occupation, the original network of military garrisons was gradually replaced by towns, and Britain grew settled and peaceful—or semipeaceful, since even at the height of imperial power, holding this unruly province required one-tenth of the Roman army. Hadrian's Wall, halfway up the island, was the outermost edge of imperial expansion, and marked, quite literally, an empire recognizing its limits.

In the year 410, when even the island's largest towns are harassed by native revolt and barbarian invasion, the Romanized citizens of Britain appeal to the emperor for aid. Shockingly, he sends word that they are on their own, and withdraws the legions from Britain; they are needed to defend Rome itself from invading Huns, Magyars, Visigoths, and Vandals, steppe tribes and upstarts whose interests run to pillage, not diplomacy. Roman society and government decamp eastward to Constantinople. And out on the periphery of empire, the web of civilization is soon so thoroughly smashed that basic skills like brickmaking and glassmaking (not to mention literacy, and silverware) do not make a comeback for nearly three hundred years. Daily life in Dark Age Britain resembles a nonstop camping trip in a Third World country. Only monks have much energy for culture. News becomes rumor; law becomes swordsmanship. No one travels; there is nothing to see, nowhere to go, no money to pay for a trip. Forests are reclaiming the old Roman fields. Bandits and wolves rule the rough tracks that were the Roman roads. Pagan ruins like Castle Copse seem uncanny places, best avoided. Cities are best avoided too; most are as dead as any radioactive site, killed by thirst once the invaders cut the urban aqueducts.

The evidence for a shift, then a decline, in Castle Copse fortunes accumulates like silt on the big trestle tables where excavation finds are brought for cleaning and cataloging. A slab of fine mosaic awkwardly patched. A cutoff in coinage. In these orts, scraps, and fragments, the archaeologist's eye decodes a portrait of a luxury villa cut off from its urbane safety net, and the death of a world. A fourth-century tale of pleasant country life—frescoes in the dining room, mosaics in the bath, jewelry for dinner parties—is brutally interrupted by fifth-century evidence of invasion and civil war. The diggers can trace how the nearby fort was reinforced, and earthen dikes erected, as the villa struggled to function in a land stripped of communications or trade. With the legions gone, and the government dissolving, Rome stays a fading memory for a generation, maybe two; people probably still wore togas, and tried to keep up their Latin. But when something wears out or breaks, no one remembers how to fix it. Three generations on, no one tries. Roman survivors, British natives, and Saxon invaders evidently decide to coexist, to intermarry, to change, in order to survive. They dry grain and butcher pigs in the great hall, set up a crude blacksmithery near the old baths. Yet four generations after the Roman legions depart, only primitive squatters' huts stand huddled in the melancholy shell of the villa on the hill.

At the largest outdoor table, a Stanford professor and half a dozen undergraduates use their softest brushes to clean the

Wiltshire dirt from a morning's metal finds—first a series of battered but recognizable Roman horseshoes, then the elegant ta-
pered handle of a bronze spoon.

"What archaeologists did before the invention of the Baggie,
I really don't know," says a Tulane faculty member, brows-
ing through a heap of recent discoveries neatly sealed in poly-
ethylene—thick pieces of greenish glass, a beautifully carved
double-sided ivory comb, and an engraved oval bracelet of
bronze, sized for a child's wrist. I pick up a Baggie at random
and hold it to the light. Suspended within is a heart-shaped
brooch, bronze pin still intact, alight with a glittering enameled
honeycomb of indigo and ruby and grass-green. Its curving surface, sixteen hundred years old, is as perfect and delicate as a
songbird's wing.

The City of River Light

Midway through the winter of 1858, as Charles Darwin sat in his country-house study high in the Kentish Downs, finishing *On the Origin of Species*, he added a quietly inflammatory paragraph asserting that inheritance, variation, and selection—fate, chance, and destiny—form the basis of life on Earth.

It is interesting to contemplate a tangled bank, clothed with plants of many kinds, with birds singing in the bushes, with various insects flitting about, and with worms crawling through the damp earth, and to reflect that these elaborately constructed forms, so different from one another, and dependent upon each other in so complex a manner, have all been produced by laws acting around us. These laws, taken in the largest sense, being Growth with Reproduction; Inheritance which is almost implied by reproduction; Variability from the indirect and direct action of the conditions of life, and from use and disuse; a Ratio of Increase so high as to lead to a

Struggle for Life, and as a consequence to Natural Selection, entailing Divergence of Character and the Extinction of less-improved forms.

From Darwin's image of the tangled bank all modern Western environmentalism descends: the concept of the food web, the belief that nature is a complex community that humans can ignore, or deny, or exploit, but never escape. But then his language darkens, summoning the relentless cycles of breeding and loss.

Thus, from the war of nature, from famine and death, the most exalted object which we are capable of conceiving, namely, the production of the higher animals, directly follows. There is grandeur in this view of life, with its several powers, having been originally breathed by the Creator into a few forms or into one; and that, whilst this planet has gone cycling on according to the fixed law of gravity, from so simple a beginning endless forms most beautiful and most wonderful have been, and are being, evolved.

Confirmed urbanites might argue that the only antidote to so much turbulent nature is the city, the built environment. Yet even the urban promise that one can choose a life, and change a life, cannot keep a citydweller (or a city) safe from extinctions. Urban extinctions lie all around us. Take the night sky. On California's Santa Cruz Island, or in the Galapagos, you can see thirty thousand stars. From a suburban backyard, maybe three hundred. In Times Square at midnight, at best a dozen. And natural sounds survived even in cities until about fifty years ago,

when the horse was pushed out of urban life, and the segrega-
tion of human and wild began to be enforced more strongly
than any color line or religious quota. In twenty-first-century
New York, as in almost all big cities around the world, two more
extinctions are under way. One is the steady loss of urban light
and air. The other is the suppression of the life of the street.

When urban architects and metropolitan planners ask citizens what they want, rather than tell them, the responses can
undercut decades of urban theory. In suburbs and exurbs, we
want to delete *road rage* and *gridlock* from the national vocabulary. We want what urbanologists call the Five-minute Popsicle Rule: that a child can walk safely from home to buy a
Popsicle within five minutes. In cities, people want other people. Crowds to watch, shaded seating, maybe a pool or a fountain, maybe a food cart: the formula for a satisfying urban
experience has not changed much since ancient Rome. Postwar
urban-studies rebels like Jane Jacobs argued for city redesigns
that promote density, activity, and intensity over the big-box-in-
a-bare-plaza mode epitomized by the corporate towers along
Manhattan's Sixth Avenue; an active street life, they claimed, is
the secret of a successful city in any age. But colorful, satisfying,
stimulating interactions are increasingly hard to arrange in New
York, or at least in Manhattan, whose midtown streets are more
crowded than Tokyo's; whose real estate is too valuable to waste
on people; whose superbuildings now steal 80 percent of summer sunlight from side streets for blocks around. Some New
York neighborhoods unlucky enough to fall within the shadow
of a skyscraper (or six) exist in permanent shadow, permanent
chill. In parts of Manhattan, at least, urban sunshine is as extinct as the giant sloths that used to roam there.

New York space comes in three brands, but most of us know

only two. First is true public space, chiefly the nature reserves and great parks: Prospect Park and Central Park, Gateway with its ocean exposures, Jamaica Bay and its reviving wildlife, Riverside and its matchless Hudson light. Everything else is aggressively private space, the most regulated, subdivided, profit-driven landscape in history. But a third kind of New York space exists too, secretive and controversial—the hundreds of privately owned public areas where anyone is allowed to go, though the owners set the conduct rules. More than 350 such enclaves now dot the city, plazas and passages, gardens and atriums, most clustered near the residential and office high-rises of midtown and the financial district. Uptown and the outer boroughs have almost none; public spaces are born of height-lust, serious money, and the bizarre legal fiction of incentive zoning.

Incentive zoning trades bulk for benefits. We want relief at street level, the Planning Commission has told developers since 1961, oases that ease the endurance contest of city life, places where people can eat a sandwich, rest sore feet, read a paper, or rock the baby under a tree for free, without fear, and without trekking twenty blocks, or fifty, to a public park. Give us that much each time you build—infuse the private realm with public interest, as the lawyers say—and we'll grant some very nice bonus floor space up above; how can you refuse? Few did, few do: each dollar spent on street-level public amenities can yield developers up to fifty dollars of profit in return. Over time, the profit ratio nears one hundred to one. The stampede for bonus footage has ruthlessly shaped Manhattan's skyline and streetscape. Bonusable spaces have been called a capitalist triumph for the common good, a smart idea betrayed, a public-policy morality play, an environmental tragedy, a devil's bargain.

And the bargain with the public? "Maybe thirty of New York's public spaces, one in ten, remain truly distinctive. Twenty-three percent, or about seventy spaces, are utilitarian, barely. The other two hundred? Two-thirds of the city's privately owned public spaces, most of them outdoors, are unusable. Miserable. Appalling." Jerrold Kayden is stalking down West Forty-third Street, denouncing as he goes. Tall and intent, with thinning sandy hair and a loping gait, Kayden is a Harvard professor of urban design, a product of Harvard and Harvard Law by way of Westchester, the son of a real estate investor and a theater composer. He dodged wild dogs and gunfire to teach Armenia's government the charms of condos, survived revolution in Katmandu when writing environmental statutes there, and spent three years as a USAID emissary to Ukraine, coaxing a new nation to accept the idea of private property ("They still resist certain basic concepts," he admits, "like ownership"). Research in New York, on New York, he thought, would be a relief. It's not. Politely, relentlessly, Kayden treks from one privately owned public space to another (his personal best is twenty-three in one day), exercising at each his legal right to enter and enjoy. Some visits are delights: the communal sculpture plaza at First and Eightieth, or Citicorp's silvery atrium. But other stops mean abusive doormen and aggressive corporate security. Guards shout at him, swear at him, chase him, order him to turn off his tape recorder, and threaten to call management, or the police. When searching Buildings Department back rooms for officially filed public-space plans, he's found instead empty fifths of gin in empty file bins.

The W. R. Grace Building. Sixth and Forty-third. Built 1971; public amenity an open-air plaza. Even during a midweek lunch hour, its grim bare sweep of travertine is the emptiest spot for blocks around. Kayden shudders. "This space actively repels," he announces, inspecting a consumptive spruce. In its dry soil old crack-vial caps glint daffodil, violet, grass-green. "Look around! *Where is everyone?* Grace used to be deeply scary; now it's embalmed. Decent plantings would help. A water feature. A miniature golf course. *Anything.*"

Grace Plaza is a dinosaur among public spaces, built in incentive zoning's first age (1961–74), when Le Corbusier ruled the earth, and the city granted developers ten free square feet of floor space for each square foot of plaza created—in the bazaar of urban air rights, a wondrous deal, resulting chiefly in a rash of very tall buildings on very bare plazas, like the monstrous slabs still lining Sixth Avenue. "Developers slapped down a little terrazzo, called it an amenity," says Kayden, deflecting a stray burger wrapper with one tan wingtip. "A cynic, and I'm not one, would call it bribing developers to do things in the public interest." And what a bribe. In the program's first eleven years, $3.8 million went to adding public-use areas onto commercial buildings, creating 7.8 million bonus square feet. At a net value of $24 per square foot, New York's developers acquired $187 million in pure profit. If they rent or sell their free square footage, then, now, forever, the profits are gravy. What does the public get, in return for sacrificing light and air? "Not nearly enough," Kayden says, consulting his checklist.

"Building owners can be amazing," he adds. "They'll swear—*swear*—an area is private. They'll discourage use by letter-of-the-law design: the perpetually shaded plaza, the grudgingly calipered tree, the official signage artfully obscured in vines. They'll take away required chairs, as the Parker Meridian Hotel did, claiming free seating attracts undesirables." Some owners simply rely on big sharp spikes to keep the public out of public spaces. At the J. P. Stevens tower on Sixth Avenue, rows of serrated metal adorn every sittable surface. "Free profits for this? It's an outrage!" says Kayden as we rise with undignified speed from the spiky ledges. "Developers are consenting adults. It's not like someone put a gun to their head and said, 'Accept a million-dollar floor-space bonus, or else.' "

The quest for solid-gold air drives the history of New York public space. At the turn of the century, the city faced a choice: should it try to look like Paris or Rome, a series of harmonious outdoor rooms, or should its model be Chicago's jagged skyline, where height is an index of power, and a city's air the new frontier? No contest: the Chicago-style steel skeleton meant that even small lots could pile more and more stories atop each square foot of ground. Architects like Louis Sullivan warned of dehumanizing congestion, of overdevelopment for its own sake, but the famously corrupt Tammany administration stifled reforms (one eventual result: the 1911 Triangle Shirtwaist fire). By the 1920s private developers were putting skyscrapers in the financial district, then the garment district, then midtown. The city fought back, first by demanding setbacks for tall buildings (which is why the Chrysler and Empire State Buildings have ziggurat designs), and then with a 1961 zoning act establishing a floor area ratio, or FAR, for all parts of the city—in effect, a limit on building bulk.

Developers howled. But to save a withering street life, the city kept trying to enlist private-sector beautification help. Let's try plazas! Let's try making Madison Avenue a pedestrian mall! Let's try—turning air into cash! The city's 1916 zoning law, the nation's first, had made New York property three-dimensional, allowing developers and lawyers to conquer, own, and trade the very air, as environmental historian Theodore Steinberg observes; twentieth-century Manhattan colonized airspace, industrialized it, allowed its rights to take a cab uptown. Air transfers preserved landmarks like Grand Central, but also let the Pan Am/MetLife building block the view up and down Park Avenue. By purchasing Tiffany's air rights, Trump Tower soared. Throughout the seventies and eighties, the powerful synergy of air rights and bonus spaces made the city grow far taller, its streets far darker. (In the words of Donald Trump's architect, Der Scutt, "If you want sunlight, move to Kansas.")

Attempting to legislate niceness, the city altered public-spaces rules, urged on by veteran citywatcher W. H. Whyte (author of *The Organization Man*). Whyte used time-lapse footage of urban behavior to confound planners' antiseptic assumptions. Live citizens, he discovered, yearn to lounge, snack, and crowd-watch. Big bare plazas bore them rigid. So the code was tightened, reducing bonus space while raising amenity demands. New requirements for developers included food kiosks, comfortable benches, freestanding chairs, bike racks, drinking fountains, and trees actually planted in the ground. The definition of "public amenity" widened too. Subway-station improvements, dance studios, day-care centers, low-income housing, arcades, atria, through-block passages, even climbing walls, earned bonus floorspace for developers throughout the eighties, the era architectural historian Gregory Gilmartin terms "that mad apogee of incentive zoning . . . when the city sold the sky for fire-sale prices."

Escaping a rain shower, Kayden and I dodge into a West Forties shopping atrium. The public seating alcove is packed, but tranquil; a young man in dreadlocks and a silver-haired woman in a sari smile and nod over sack lunches, adolescents flirt, and businessmen in stocking feet play Tetris on their laptops. "From a larger city-planning point of view, these Eighties atria drain life from the street. But this one's well done," says Kayden, hanging perilously over the escalator rail. "No, I take it back. See that? A definite commercial intrusion." Along two sides of the atrium's lowest level, white-clothed tables spill out beyond a restaurant entrance. To the civilian eye, the area seems part of the restaurant, but it's actually public space, deftly transformed into moneymaking footage. "We wouldn't actually chase people out if they sat there without ordering," admits the manager when pressed, but neither is anyone advertising that these tables are illegally trespassing on public space. "It's trattoria creep, eroding, nibbling, pushing at what's not theirs, betting no one will notice," grumbles Kayden. "Public spaces have no rules, no case law. Each owner, manager, guard, attendant, and maître d' interprets the meaning of the deal independently, and the conclusions are different each time."

Coops and apartments can be just as nervy. At the Plaza Tower, 118 East Sixtieth, a half-moon driveway embraces a pocket garden. "How the hell is this a publicly accessible space?" hisses Kayden as we crawl across the bumper of a white stretch limo. Along the sidewalk rises a low pink marble divider, top edge honed to a vicious angle. Two burly doormen wave us off. "Who are you? You can't sit there. Too many Yuppies tried to sit there, so we put that wall in. Leave. Now." Is this privately owned public space? They are icily, antiphonally clear. "This is—" "Private." "Private." "Private." "Private." "Even to stand here—" "You gotta live in the building."

On to the Brevard, 245 East Fifty-fourth, a 445-unit coop.

We sidle past a dozen uncollected garbage bags to find the public-space plaza, its air ripe with hot-grease fumes, its amenities a Dumpster, a barely trickling drinking fountain, trash in the planters, rusty chairs, a public-space sign stuck behind a bush, and a dead water wall adorned with coils of barbed wire. In one corner, a ragged, filthy man rocks and stares. Kayden groans. "A classic example of why self-regulation is meaningless." And difficult: the building has gone through three management companies in four years. The building supervisor, who used to deal with a hundred homeless people a night when managing the New York Coliseum, does his best. "That plaza is a definite security problem, what with partying kids, dogs, and street people. East Siders don't want to deal with any of that. And the original owners are long gone."

"There's no institutional memory," explains Kayden as we head toward Fifth. "The developers cash out, and no tenant or condo owner wants to hear that a high-priced courtyard is legally open to screaming strangers, just because someone wangled a bonus back in the Nixon administration. In every New York public space now, two legitimate visions clash: that public spaces are for everyone's enjoyment, and that some publics are more desirable than others."

Paley Park, on East Fifty-third Street, a few steps off Fifth Avenue. A vest-pocket park on the site of the old Stork Club, given to the city in 1977 by CBS founder William Paley. Bonus square footage: none. Like the Rockefeller-funded Greenacre Park on Fifty-first Street, it is a gift to the people of New York. We step up, away from the street, toward the sound of rushing water, and in less than a second are in a calmer world. "This is a *great* public space. Simple, quiet, no gimmicks, no litter," Kayden murmurs. "The water wall blocks city blare, there's plenty of movable seating, even birdsong." Some paint is peeling, and the ivy looks sparse, but three dozen visitors contentedly read, knit, catnap, play cards, and watch the twenty-foot cascade. An attendant carefully empties trash cans, while the refreshment stand dispenses hot dogs (no longer Mr. Paley's special recipe, but still first-rate). Each person who leaves the little park is visibly refreshed. For the first time in hours, Kayden smiles. "Look at the faces," he murmurs. "Look at the *faces*."

About half of United States cities now encourage the public-private partnership through Manhattan-style incentive zoning. In San Francisco, rooftop observatories for tourists resulted; in Anchorage, heated walkways. But New York's collection of public spaces is the nation's first and largest, *if* you can find them. Ask developers to maintain their bonus areas, to honor their deal, and reactions range from outright defiance to bare compliance to intelligent cooperation. Profits are hardly evil, any developer will counter. We're forced to build tall because Manhattan keeps so much acreage archaically zoned for manufacturing. It's hard to do business in a city that doesn't follow its own laws, or know its own mind. Struggles between developers and the city can transcend administrations, even decades. In 1984, aware that Grace Plaza had become a hangout for the homeless and the drug trade, the owners left up a construction fence blocking the entire area much longer than necessary. Incensed, the city made them take it down. A five-million-dollar remodeling was then proposed: café, bistro, health-food bar, bookstall, flower stand, food carts, a stage, sculptures, a fountain, even a giant video screen for soaps and old movies. Unless you keep rigidly set hours, city lawyers replied, we may sue you. The owners resisted, saying they feared high-handed enforcement. Stalemate. A generation later, Grace Plaza remains a sad blank spot in midtown's densest stretch, though plans are underway to add a glass pavilion, more benches, more trees. As architectural critic Ada Louise Huxtable points out, the core purpose of zoning "within constitutional limits, is to make a city a fit place to live; concern for light, air, health, safety, and beauty is supposed to be at the heart of zoning law. The poker players have forgotten."

To Jerrold Kayden, New York is increasingly an inward-turning city; not good, because a sense of place is essential to civic decency, and civic self. "Cities by nature feature lots of interaction, lots of distraction, people flinging themselves together and trying to be happy," he points out, turning onto Third Avenue. "Step out the door, and you're forcibly democratized. Let a city decline, and it hemorrhages, first to the suburbs, then to walled and gated and guarded suburbs. Incentive spaces are supposed to preserve a sound common street life. Mess with that contract, twist urban zoning for commercial gain, and you get grotesque misuse of the law. Separate yourself, and that's the end of a civil society."

At 767 Third, the outdoor public space proves minimalist but neat—sturdy tables and chairs, a modest brick plaza, and on the wall a gigantic chess game. Each week, the pieces are redeployed to enact a single move, playing out over the months and years the great games of history. But as we try to sit, a guard and his Rottweiler stare balefully from the building's lobby, and a blond woman in an Armani jacket rushes toward us, screaming "Get out! This is private property!" before vanishing into the rush-hour crowd. Kayden turns to follow, dodging between moving cabs. "Jerrold Kayden, urban ranger," he calls to me over his shoulder. "I want my grave to say, 'He went to all the public spaces in New York.'" But his quarry has disappeared. Sunset is nearly here, and Kayden has a dozen spaces yet to inspect. The last I see of him, he is heading west, walking his urgent private beat, inspecting the health and mood of gingkos, contemplating lawsuits, and stopping only to reposition a public chair here and there, in order to catch the last of the light.

Rising Tide

Urban experts love the future, but rarely think ahead. Half a century seems to be an especially challenging span for the city-watcher's imagination: near enough to be personal, distant enough to baffle, or seduce. Consider the New York of the early 1950s. Its air would seem sooty to us, partly because of the thousands of coal furnaces and coal fires still in use, partly because New York had one million manufacturing jobs then, versus barely a quarter-million today. But the sidewalks, even in the toughest neighborhoods, would look stunningly clean. Corporate offices in this lost metropolis use mimeograph machines and slide rules. Libraries have vast wooden card catalogs. Hotel rooms have keys. Broadway theater is at its joyous peak, even though a good seat costs $2.50. The old Ladies' Mile of retail shopping has moved north on Fifth Avenue to the prosperous blocks between Central Park and the East Forties, a phalanx of department stores with names like law firms—Bonwit Teller, Bergdorf Goodman, Lord & Taylor, Peck & Peck. These stay crowded all day with female shoppers whose urban dress code is exacting and absolute: skirts and high heels, white gloves and hats, serious girdles. Horse-drawn delivery wagons can still be spotted, even in Manhattan, and in fall every American city, New York included, fills with the smell of burning leaves.

Urban improvement here seems a sunny, rational crusade. To improve transportation, you enlarge passenger-rail stations, obviously, and (in Manhattan) the West Side ocean-liner docks. Commercial prop-plane travel is still a novelty, like television, and no one has heard of an interstate highway system, though Columbia University president Dwight Eisenhower of Manhattan wants to change that, should he become president of the United States and no longer president of Columbia University. To ensure industrial progress, defense plants, chemical tank farms, and pesticide factories remain solid bets. For in-town commuting, many American cities are scrapping their sturdy, unglamorous streetcars and investing in buses. To encourage urban commerce, they want more skyscrapers, but also good Western Union service, a touch of slum cleanup, and perhaps some new hospitals, with elm-shaded grounds, capacious fallout shelters, and Vitaglass windows for the obstetrics and polio wards, both of which are getting a lot of business.

The bad guesses of the 1950s remain visible from almost any window in America. When metropolitan residents of 2050 consider the state of the nation circa 2000, built and natural, they too may waver between nostalgia and rage. In some ways, 2050 is already here. Its shade trees are our garden-center saplings, and almost 1 million 1950 babies will live to sit under them as centenarians. (The winner of the 2048 presidential race may already be in day care.) In 2050, there will be twice as many of us in the United States—nearly 500 million. One-quarter of the population will be Hispanic. Among school-age children, whites will be a minority. The needs and wants of the Cottontop Nation will dominate public policy and private convenience; an astonishing 20 percent of the population will be over sixty-five. And half of the New York population may have been born outside the United States, making the city a true world capital, though of no particular country.

What will New York look like, fifty years hence? Professional citywatchers promote conflicting visions of the ultimate city's future: New York as cybercity, as tourist city, as dystopian battleground, as the new Venice. Visions and scenarios, restorations and evolutions, abound. So do predictions of decline and fall. Some commentators, like Los Angeles architect Peter Katz, a leading theorist of the New Urbanism movement, reject a *Bladerunner* future of civic chaos and decay. "Computer networks will never replace community. Cities of the future will look and function pretty much like the best cities of the past." Kenneth Frampton, a professor of architecture at Columbia, foresees debilitating entropy. "All the indicators suggest that the megalopolis will continue to expand without constraint, ultimately leaving in its wake the fragmented detritus of worn-out stock and infrastructure, not to mention people. . . . Hence the familiar bombed-out expanses of Detroit, Buffalo, Houston, et cetera."

To give up the dream of a truly cool future may be hardest of all. For much of the twentieth century, experts and citizens agreed that our destiny was urban, but conspicuously disagreed on rethinking the city. "The big city is no longer modern," said Frank Lloyd Wright in 1923. "The city is an attack on nature," announced Le Corbusier, meaning it as a compliment. Pop and high culture offered us dozens of urbanized imaginings, from *Brave New World* to *Star Trek* to *Mad Max*. Some were idyllic, some decidedly dystopian, and not a few, like Wright's designs for a Broadacre City and a mile-high tower, worked better as morality plays than as actual cityscapes. We have toyed with space cities, underwater cities, and cities built on giant landfills (which turned out to be true, at least for Tokyo, New York, and Hong Kong).

In 1955, California's Disneyland opened a relentlessly up-beat Tomorrowland section, featuring the House of the Future, sponsored by Monsanto, designed at MIT. Termite-proof and book-free, it advertised a domestic paradise of microwave cooking and push-button phones, atomic food preservation and floating furniture. ("When Walt Disney was alive, the future was candy-coated," a Disney executive admitted recently. "We were all going to have our own flying saucers and dress in gold lamé.") Likewise, the most popular exhibit at New York's 1939 World's Fair was a ride called the Futurama, sponsored by GM, which tantalized Depression-weary Americans with the splendors of 1960, when all cancers would be curable, all cars super-fast, and all seventy-year-old women guaranteed a perfect complexion. Taking notes in the crowd was E. B. White. "I liked 1960 in purple light," he wrote, "going a hundred miles an hour around impossible turns ever onward toward the certified cities of the flawless future. It wasn't till I passed an apple orchard and saw the trees, each blooming under its own canopy of glass, that I perceived even the General Motors dream, as dreams often do, left some questions unanswered about the future. The apple tree of Tomorrow, abloom under its inviolate hood, makes you stop and wonder. How will the little boy climb it? Where will the little bird build its nest?"

Rising Tide

Imagined or limited-edition futures are rarely a match for their serendipitous cousin, the future that happens while you're making other plans. But the professional literatures of architecture, information technology, geography, urban and regional development, political science, ecology, and cultural studies seethe with suggestions for the urban future, and Greater New York is a frequent test case, since New Yorkers are like people who have lived in a cluttered house for decades: you can deep-clean, you can remodel, you can ignore the mess, you can declare it an artwork in progress. The only thing you can't do is move next door and try again.

The cybercity may be New York's easiest reincarnation to accept, if you don't mind losing the Manhattan skyline. By 2050, skyscrapers will almost certainly be an extinct species, preserved for tourists or remade into housing; skyscraper construction has already halted in almost every United States city except Manhattan's West Side, which is not yet (by local standards) built out. Tall commercial buildings do continue to rise, but in Malaysia and Korea and Hong Kong. Of the world's hundred most recent superbuildings—sixty stories or more—only two were North American. In 1950, it made sense to concentrate your workers in one tall structure; now, the borderless metropolis, driven by the 24-7 desires of infotech, has begun to make the New York commuter another endangered species, or else a retrained one: in a few decades, the dominant pattern may be "live in the city/work in the suburbs." And a new metropolitan underclass—the unwired—is already forming; Detroit has twice the population of Denver, but only one-third as much Internet backbone capacity; greater Philadelphia is a poorly wired city compared to the much smaller Miami/Fort Lauderdale region. Wired winners include the Bay Area, Washington, D.C.,

Chicago, Dallas, and Seattle. In Manhattan, midtown, Wall Street, the Upper West Side, and Silicon Alley are decidedly on-line, but not Harlem or Washington Heights or the Lower East Side. Eastern Queens is, the middle-class immigrant neighborhoods especially; Brooklyn, the Bronx, and Staten Island are not. Urban epidemics of the next decades are being redefined to include cyberpathologies as well as rashes of broken windows and child abuse and drug-resistant STDs. Researchers are already mapping the new trouble spots: the blocks with the fewest PCs and Internet connections, the stretches of the city that log on least, the neighborhoods most given to on-line gambling. Some would like to map auto densities as well, arguing that the auto is a manmade parasite more destructive of animal and human habitat than any plague in history, and its increase has been pandemic: 50 million cars in the world in 1950, 350 million in 1980, more than 500 million today. (Rome, Oslo, Singapore, and Amsterdam all ban or heavily tax cars now, at least in the center of town.)

The green city as a New York future will be a tougher sell. The city has thousands of acres of brownfields it can't build on, by federal fiat; the land is too polluted to be safe for human habitation. By 2050, phytoremediation may have helped reclaim these areas: many common plants, some native, some alien, can clean city earth and urban water with great efficiency, given the chance. More than four hundred species are known pollution-eaters, a cheap, quick, ingenious fix for a profound urban problem. Mulberry trees and Indian mustard love heavy metals and contaminants. Crabgrass and hybrid poplars are even more talented at urban healing. If plants had a union, New York would be a far cleaner town. But Philadelphia and Trenton are trying urban agriculture (already big in Germany, India, and Canada).

Florida and California have invested in manmade marshes and artificial wetlands to filter urban pollution. Some green fixes are indirect: in the 1970s, Portland, Oregon, saw urban rot and suburban sprawl and established an urban-growth boundary, which has yielded a lively downtown and a healthy urban ecology, as city land-development patterns evolved from use-and-abandon to use-and-reuse.

Other places employ grade-school science to solve billion-dollar problems. With Environmental Protection Agency encouragement, the city of Chicago is planting rooftop gardens and (like Baton Rouge and Salt Lake City) urging public and private buildings to switch to pale-colored roofing. It's also investing in street trees. Reflective surfaces and extra greenery cool the urban heat island by seven or eight degrees, providing shade, lowering air temperature. Three trees per city house can cut an air-conditioning bill by 30 percent; install enough trees near urban-pollution sources and blacktop deserts, and you can skip building that extra power plant. As an urban economy grows, urban trees tend to fall; twenty years ago, New York, like Washington, was a far leafier town. New York recruits the most resilient species known for its 2.5 million city trees—honey locust, willow oak, linden, Japanese zelkova, hybrid sycamore—but one-fifth or more are overcome, well before maturity, by the combined assaults of exhaust, dog urine, air pollution, salt shock, and acid rain. Trees in the forest live thirty years longer than trees on the street, at least a New York street. Manhattan trees are killed off fastest. (Paris, on the other hand, inserts a computer chip in each of its ninety thousand street specimens and coordinates their watering, pruning, and feeding via a database.)

Larger public experiments in urban greening—more walkable communities, more light rail, more public green space, better traffic-calming—have been spotty at best in this supremely crowded region, whose interest in ecotopian experiment is historically limited to putting sprouts on bagels. Area developers, though, are keeping an eye on a new luxury highrise in lower Manhattan's Battery Park City. Designed to be energy-efficient, recycling-friendly, solar-powered, and anti-allergy, it even re-uses gray water from building washing machines and showers for building toilets—and in the process reaps a ton of environmental tax credits from the state. But given the New York tradition of strained relations with nature, any number of carrots and sticks may be required to alter the collective mental map so that natural areas are more than cartographic white space, toxic hotspots have a name and history, and environmental power relations (why *do* the city's poorest areas have the most landfills?) are as clearly etched in the urban mind as the best routes from Forty-second Street to La Guardia.

When in doubt, downsize. New York is an excellent candidate for a breakup, actually, since Queens has repeatedly expressed interest in unhooking from New York City, Brooklyn never quite lost its separate identity—culturally if not legally—and Staten Island has already held half a dozen votes on secession, each closer than the next, claiming it would rather join New Jersey than be a landfill site and labor pool for prodigal Manhattan. New Jersey has already gone to court to get title to some or all of Liberty Island and Ellis Island, so Staten Island would be a natural addition, since it lies far closer to Newark than to Manhattan. (Westchester County could, presumably, annex the Bronx, a prospect that thrills neither party.)

The eastern shore of Maryland, northern Maine, and Michi-

gan's Upper Peninsula have all investigated becoming separate
states of late, as the San Fernando Valley has hoped to become
the nation's sixth-largest city, not merely upper L.A. As old urban alliances fade, as New York's failing infrastructure and in-
creasing congestion and worsening heat index lessen its raucous
charms, there's always the risk that the urban party may move
to the Sunbelt or the Bay Area. New York Life has already sent
its data-processing operation to Ireland, as the back-office oper-
ations of Salomon Brothers have gone to Tampa. Companies of
the future are expected to be even more footloose.

The Regional Planning Association, grown soberer and
more inclusive as the twentieth century progressed, now sees
just two probable futures for the New York of 2020: either a
crumbling core, with near-total transportation paralysis and de-
teriorating air and water, or else a genuinely livable city in the
style of Toronto or Santiago or Paris, infrastructure rehabbed,
environment protected—a deindustrializing city transformed
into a sustainable one. In its previous reports (1929 and 1968),
the association considered uncontrolled growth New York's
greatest problem; their new findings spotlight decline. Ignore
it, they say, and "the next 20 years will represent the final chap-
ter in a story of prosperity and momentum that dates to the settlement of Manhattan."

Between 1980 and 2000, New York unexpectedly morphed
from imperial city into tourist city. Tourism, like information
processing, has become an economic force to rival the heavy
industry of the past. Some cities sense this, others don't, but
when urban areas compete for the international tourist trade,
they evolve in three distinct ways. Resort cities are created ex-
pressly for consumption by out-of-towners, like Las Vegas and

Cancun. Tourist-historic cities, like Prague, Charleston, and Boston, offer a mix of present culture and past atmosphere. Converted cities construct a tourist bubble, as Baltimore has done with its Harborplace/Camden Yards district, an area that functions as a tourist reservation as well as a tourist theme park, keeping visitors cordoned and cosseted while simultaneously warding off threatening locals and other unpleasant urban sights, like rat packs or trash-to-steam plants. New York is becoming a converted city, decidedly cleaner and safer than New York in 1980, from the perkily remade Times Square and theater district to the blocks of new housing in the South Bronx. By 2050, barring a return of its lost industrial base, New York may well evolve from a converted city to a tourist-historic one, dotted with charmingly restored landmarks from the late twentieth century. A Forest Hills gas station, for the amusement of a fuel-cell future. A Loehmann's discount clothing outlet. A RadioShack. A Krispy Kreme doughnut outlet. Trump Tower.

The out-of-control supercity has been a widely fantasized future for New York since the 1950s. Like Cavafy's barbarians, it would solve *so* many problems. The Giuliani years depressed the market for New York dystopias, particularly the vision of a New York segregated into equally hostile and well-armed camps of rich and poor: the privileged locked into gated compounds by night and moving about the daylight city in anxious convoys, as in the London of Dickens or Pepys, the underclass roving Park Avenue seeking whom they may devour. But if New York has deflected this particular future of urban chaos and misrule, Moscow and Rio have not. By 2050, 80 percent of humanity will live in urban settings, and population growth in conglomerations like Lagos, Dacca, and São Paulo should be extraordinary; even if the growth curve slows, the World Bank reminds us, by 2010—2010!—a total of 1.4 billion citydwellers will live without basic services. (By 2030, nearly 6 billion of us will be slumdwellers. North America now has three of the five First World supercities—New York, Mexico City, Los Angeles, Tokyo, London. By 2050, not one of the world's twenty largest urban areas will be in the developed nations.)

Some urbanists point meaningfully to Tokyo as a well-managed megacity; others whisper that a 2050 visit even to New York or L.A. will require a special travel kit of antibiotics, insecticide, and barter goods like peanut butter or batteries. If our enthusiasm for exurbia slackens, it's even possible to imagine today's developments as the ghost towns of 2100, or to assume a future New York resigned to rolling power blackouts, as in New Delhi today, or to envision a Manhattan whose bedrock is honeycombed with underground shops and offices, à la Toronto, in order to use every precious foot of island. United States armed forces are already practicing for urban warfare, expected to be the dominant combat form in the new century. The New York City government is sporadically practicing too, for the bioterrorism attack predicted for some major urban area in the next decade. The Internet makes urban plagues an easy specialty. Nearly fifty Web sites are already selling lethal viruses like anthrax or smallpox in the convenient powdered (or "weaponized") form.

Yet all New York futures, triumphalist or declensionist, must eventually confront the effects of global warming on a coastal megacity. In the new century, we will see a noticeably hotter, wetter New York. Drought will alternate with bursts of extreme weather. At least two big hurricanes a year, plus more blizzards, ice storms, hailstorms, and storm surges will also join the urban scene. The New York Academy of Sciences warns that New York in 2050 will be a city with much more ozone (and thus more smog), and frequent electrical shortages. Asthma cases and heat deaths will soar. Today, bad air kills about 320 New Yorkers each year; by 2020, that number is expected to jump to nearly 2,000. New York already has the nation's worst heat-mortality rates; by 2030, they will probably double. Global warming already allows tropical mosquitoes to survive at New York's latitude, and malaria cases have been reported on Long Island, making encephalitis and dengue fever two excellent candidates for future New York public-health crises. In all the big East Coast cities, rising heat and humidity will make the warm months exceedingly soggy. But a 1999 Princeton University study predicts that the New York area will be exceptionally uncomfortable, particularly for the old, the poor, and the ill. Sunscreen won't do it; twenty-first-century New York summers will begin in April and last through October. New York in summer will feel like Atlanta does now. Atlanta will feel like Houston. Houston will resemble Sumatra. The New York heatwaves that now average fourteen days may stretch to twenty-eight or thirty days of temperatures over 100 degrees by 2020. Heatstroke, heat cramps, increased ground-level ozone, and heat exhaustion will affect millions of residents; energy demands for air-conditioning will soar in and around the Baked Apple. It will be harder to draw a full breath, harder to see across the street, harder to hold a business meeting without bouts of coughing around the table. Filters worn over the nose and mouth, as is already done in some polluted Asian cities, may become the new style trend. Climate fluctuation speeds up virus mutation. Expect more urban superviruses, and fewer effective antibiotics to combat them.

Earth, air, fire, water: in 1998 alone, natural disasters created more refugees than wars and regional conflicts, as declining soil fertility, drought, hurricanes, flooding, desertification, and deforestation drove some twenty-five million into urban shantytowns and slums. International organizations from the Red Cross to the global insurance industry expect weather-triggered superdisasters to punctuate the next century, sparked by a mix of climate change, environmental damage, and population pressures. Most of humanity lives near seacoasts; a two- or three-foot rise in ocean levels by 2050 will put Venice, San Francisco, Sydney, Vancouver, Osaka, and Tokyo waist-deep. Even the most conservative scientists consider New Orleans, already eight feet below sea level, an excellent candidate for becoming the American Venice, or perhaps the next Atlantis, should a Gulf hurricane push Lake Pontchartrain over the levees and into the city.

New York is nearly as vulnerable. Seamed with rivers, subways, and sewage-treatment systems, it is a watery city anyway; should sea level eventually increase three feet, as some academic and government forecasters expect, Battery Park City, the Rockaways, Coney Island, Alphabet City, Red Hook, Jersey City, and much of the financial district will all be drowned land. The beaches of the Hamptons will disappear. The FDR Drive and the Gowanus Expressway will need to be shored up, raised, or abandoned as the ground beneath them takes on water and turns unstable. If the tide gates at city sewage-treatment plants are submerged (as has already happened several times during especially hard rains), raw sewage will back up into New York streets. La Guardia Airport, only six feet above sea level, will have to close. Dikes may keep the runways at Kennedy and Newark open for a few decades before they too succumb. The city's 137 miles of underground subway, especially the 4, 5, and 6 trains in lower Manhattan, will rarely be usable. (During major storms, service between Brooklyn and Manhattan already feels the effects of tunnel flooding.) City curfews may become common, as repair crews work by night to clean up storm damage. And expect more traffic on Broadway in the future, since the West Side Highway will almost certainly be under water.

The Irish say that the veil over the future's face is woven by an angel of mercy. But new computer modeling studies, ordered by Congress, designed to reveal the local effects of climate change, suggest that the veil is falling away. As early as 2020, certainly by 2050, we will see islands disappear, and forests move. Ecosystems unable to migrate, like the coral reefs of Hawaii and Florida, will not survive in the warming (and increasingly polluted) oceans. Colorado will need a new state flower, since its alpine meadows will vanish with the Rocky Mountain snowpack, taking the columbine with them—and most of the water supply for Front Range cities like Denver. The New England of 2040 will have no brilliant fall foliage, and no spring sugaring. Maples will have disappeared from the United States altogether, though they will probably survive in Canada, where a thinning Arctic ice pack will doom species like polar bears but permit, at long last, a Northwest Passage. No more Maine potatoes, though; the climate is too warm, too dry. Ski resorts across the United States are closed for lack of snow.

Rising Tide

Bar Harbor is drowned, and much of Cape Cod. Nantucket and Martha's Vineyard have nearly vanished under the sea. Boston, Baltimore, and Miami are steadily losing urban acreage to the rising tides. The Florida Keys are a memory, like North Carolina's ribbon of sand, the Outer Banks. No more Jersey shore.

Try the longer view, the wider lens. During the next century, winter as we have known it will disappear in much of the United States. Trees everywhere grow faster. Cotton thrives, apples decline. More rainfall for the Southwest allows grasslands, or shrubby forests, or both, to begin retaking the Arizona and Nevada deserts, and the developers will be right behind; more water means more subdivisions. (For North America's next megacity, consider Phoenix in 2100.) The supercomputers disagree on the fate of southern forests; they may either dry into savannah, as drought and heat crack the region, or else southern rainfall will increase by 25 percent, making even bigger forests, but also nastier floods and more and harsher blizzards (think of the North Carolina floods of 1999, or the March 1996 snowstorm that shut down the East Coast from Washington, D.C., to Maine, only doubled). The cool fogs of the Pacific Northwest may vanish too, as warming offshore waters kill off the remaining salmon, and snow on Mount Rainier becomes a thing of the past. California's rainfall may drastically increase, helping crops but causing tremendous floods and landslides in urban areas. The Great Lakes will drop four to five feet. But farmers in the Midwest and the prairie provinces likely double their wheat and grain crops as the midcontinental climate warms, and warms, and warms. Minneapolis and Chicago see a startling rise in heat-related deaths. And Nebraska real estate may be the Next New Thing: in 2000, 60 percent of humanity—3.8 billion people—live along a coastline, or within a hundred miles of one; by 2030, three-fourths of the world's population may live near sea level. It's not good timing, since coastal areas suffer most from the intensified storms and rising seas of climate change, both of which erode shoreline, increase salt levels in drinking-water supplies, and encourage human migrations. ("There could be 17 million refugees from Bangladesh alone as sea levels rise," observe the editors of a New York Academy of Sciences report on New York City and global warming.) In the United States alone, 55 percent of all Americans currently live and work in 772 coastal counties; by 2025, some 75 percent of Americans will probably make their homes in coastal areas. Beach houses on stilts may become a standard design solution, albeit a temporary one, since one American beachfront house in four is expected to be lost to erosion by 2060. Atlantic coast structures are most endangered, then Gulf Coast, then Pacific.

Natural indignities worry some American cities more than others. Los Angeles and San Francisco may be due for serious earthquakes. Miami is still rebuilding from 1993's Hurricane Andrew, as Grand Forks, North Dakota, and the towns of the upper Mississippi valley continue to recover from their five-hundred-year floods. Charleston has endured a direct hurricane strike (Hugo, in 1989) and an 1886 quake felt as far away as Omaha, and Harlem. Saint Louis is nearly atop the New Madrid fault, which produced a major temblor in 1811. The 1980 eruption of Mount Saint Helens showered Portland with volcanic ash. Seattle, a three-fault town, has small earthquakes all the time, but remains well overdue for either one big shake a thousand times stronger than the 1995 earthquake that so damaged Kobe, Japan, or maybe a decade of small but destructive shudders—area seismologists aren't sure. (Until they decide, the Seattle Emergency Management director suggests that residents should keep extra drinking water and a crowbar on hand, just in case.)

So far, New York has dodged urban catastrophe. Three significant earthquakes have struck the region in the last three centuries. The most recent, in 1884, was felt as far away as Ohio; Columbia University seismologists believe another is possible, especially since the Newark Basin, encircling the city, is bordered by two sets of increasingly active faults. Manhattan is full of fault lines. One runs under Broadway. Another cuts from the West Fifties down to the Lower East Side. A third snakes from the Columbia University campus under Mount Sinai Hospital to Yorkville and the Upper East Side. New Yorkers who take comfort in the bedrock beneath Manhattan should remember that maybe a quarter of the island is really manmade landfill, which turns very bouncy under seismic stress. And the outer boroughs, Queens and the eastern Bronx especially, are built on geological Jell-O: soft soil that even a mild quake could liquefy. Even a modest New York temblor (a 5.5, say) would crack bridges, flood tunnels, burst water and gas mains, and make urban firefighting—or urban rescue—exceptionally hard. The city's antique water pipes are unlikely to stand the strain of any earthquake. The flooded streets would be a mass of fallen bricks, concrete slabs, and abandoned cars. New York's steel-frame towers, built to give with the wind, are the best structures in which to ride out an initial shock, but ten minutes postquake, the skyscraper fires would likely begin. All this, of course, assumes a moderate earthquake on a warm, clear day.

Should a large quake hit New York in winter, the misery index would be infinitely higher. One Columbia University study suggests that a 6.0 quake centered five miles from City Hall would mean more than a thousand deaths, ten thousand injuries, and a hundred thousand New Yorkers left homeless.

Tidal waves and hurricanes are likelier natural events in a coastal megacity. A tsunami did hit in 1964 after an earthquake far offshore, but hardly anyone noticed, since by the time the great wave reached the city it was only a foot high. The collapse of an underwater formation nearer the coast, however, or the release of an undersea dome of pressurized water (like the recently discovered examples off northern New Jersey) would destroy about half of Brooklyn, and perhaps a third of Queens. But city officials' greatest fear remains the Category 4 or Category 5 hurricane that strikes Manhattan during rush hour at high tide. Epic hurricanes have passed over the city many times, but in less populous years: 1635, 1815, 1821, and 1893. The 1821 hurricane was especially dramatic: a storm surge rose thirteen feet in one hour, pushing East River waters up over the lower end of Manhattan Island and into the Hudson. The eye of the no-name storm of 1938, which killed six hundred people in New York and New England, was seventy-five miles from the city but still knocked out subway service throughout the Bronx and above Manhattan's Fifty-ninth Street. Hurricane Gloria brushed the city in 1985, Hurricane Floyd in 1999. By 2100, the superstorms that have struck two or three times a century may arrive every five years.

The Army Corps of Engineers and the National Weather Service have discovered that the seacoast where New York and New Jersey meet is perfectly sloped and shaped to amplify the effects of a direct hit by even a modest hurricane. The Corps, in fact, believes that New York is the most dangerous storm-surge area in the nation. A direct encounter with a Category 3 hurricane would mean a twenty-foot jump in water level at the Statue of Liberty, a thirty-foot shift at Jamaica Bay and Kennedy Airport. Private planes and corporate jets would float like bathtub toys. Larger aircraft might be pushed into the terminal by the stormwaters' force. If a storm surge of seventeen feet in one hour arrived in the city, the Brooklyn-Battery Tunnel would flood entirely. The peak storm surge at the Lincoln Tunnel would be more than twenty-eight feet. Water would rush into the subways through sidewalk vents in Manhattan and Brooklyn. The Hoboken PATH trains would flood too, (exactly as happened in 1992, when a train had to be rescued from a nor'easter storm surge. It took officials ninety minutes to rescue nineteen people). Three and a half million commuters arrive in midtown every day; in a storm, a great many of them would be trying to get home through New York tunnels on trains and buses—you do the math. The rest of the storm surge would rush into lower Manhattan. The World Trade Center lobby would be a reflecting pool. Heavy Staten Island flooding could even break open the lower levels of Fresh Kills, releasing methane, toxins, and millions of tons of elderly New York garbage.

If a hurricane strikes, New York gets very wet, for a while. But sea-level rise from global warming will bring the city permanent change. The Army Corps of Engineers has already estimated how much it would cost to keep the five boroughs dry. To give New York urban levees, the price is about one million dollars per waterfront mile. Constructing floodgates, sea walls, and a locks system for the harbor, blocking off the Narrows, the Arthur Kill, and the Whitestone Bridge area, would be far pricier—perhaps one hundred million dollars altogether, probably far more. A great deal of the Hudson River would have to be diverted into the Delaware, of course, but that's progress. If a major engineering project is not undertaken, flooding from global warming, or from a serious hurricane, would put certain New York areas—not to mention a number of low-lying Superfund sites—at pronounced risk. In Queens, these include the Rockaway peninsula, Broad Channel, Howard Beach, and West Hamilton Beach. On Staten Island: New Dorp Beach, Oakwood Beach, Foxwood Beach, Great Kills, Tottenville. In Brooklyn: Coney Island, Brighton Beach, Manhattan Beach, and Sheepshead Bay. In the Bronx: Edgewater Park, Silver Beach, Locust Point, Classon Point, Throgs Neck. Manhattan should prepare to be very wet from a few blocks below Union Square down to Battery Park City and the South Street Seaport area, and from midtown south to the lower West Side and Wall Street. On the East Side, the entire FDR Drive, the Lower East Side, and much of the Village—the once and future wetlands of Minetta Water—are all vulnerable territory.

Even an optimist's view of New York in 2050 needs to include certain new landmarks, and new losses. The Brooklyn and lower Manhattan subways will almost certainly be closed five decades hence, and all the city's coastal roadways and train tracks long since flooded. A dusty, battered Central Park will be inhabited chiefly by junk trees and weedy species. Oaks, wildflowers, and songbirds will be gone, or nearly so, from the new, overheated New York, though other, more adaptable varieties of urban wildlife should spread and thrive, from the harbor herons to the midtown coyotes. Under-city floods will drive millions of New York rats to the surface, but rats are eminently adaptable, and should enjoy the incessant sewage backups along the avenues of midtown. And New York 2050 will have become a fine haven for warm-climate insects of every sort, from yellow jackets and killer bees to Formosan termites, fire ants, and a great many mosquitoes, many of them carrying viruses, some familiar, others emerging. Every year, as the waters rise, New York's heavily humanized landscape will also become more clearly a city of islands, the Dorian Gray edition of the kindly archipelago the Lenape knew.

All worlds end. Death, as Darwin knew, is the mother of evolution. It's worth remembering that we are in what geologists call the third great Ice Age (recessive phase). Fifteen thousand years ago, ice covered New York. Fifteen thousand years from now, global warming notwithstanding, the ice will return. If anyone is still living in the New York area, massive evacuations will be necessary as the glaciers crawl south once more, and the skyscraper ruins fall to the advancing ice edge: the witty Chippendale cornice of the Sony Building, the silvery Art Deco turret of the Chrysler Building, the zeppelin-tether pinnacle of the Empire State, and, last of all, the double towers of the World Trade Center at Manhattan's tip. If, in the meantime, greenhouse gases or natural climatological cycles, or both, continue to encourage the West Antarctic ice sheet to melt, as the North Pole ice pack, like the Greenland ice reserve, is melting now, even conservative projections suggest that ocean levels will rise enough to flood most of Florida, and all of the Mississippi and Nile Deltas, and to return one-tenth of Manhattan to the sea.

Day and Night

A large-scale study underwritten by the European Union in late 2000 strongly suggests that global warming will profoundly alter landscape and climate from the Mediterranean to Scandinavia in the next half century. Dry regions will turn drier, wet areas wetter. In Britain, look for mild winters and heavy floods; hot summers and droughts will become the UK norm, so much so that in the south of England, vineyards and sunflowers may become cash crops. In Austria and Switzerland, alpine plants and species will die, ski resorts will be abandoned, glaciers will melt, and mountaintops will collapse as permafrost retreats. Finland's tundra will disappear, replaced by birch and pine. In Sweden, forests will grow up to seventy percent faster, pushing north toward the former Arctic. Salmon will vanish from the Loire and sturgeon from the Black Sea as Europe's rivers warm. Nuclear power stations will become endangered species too, for lack of cooling water. All around the Mediterranean, coastal wetlands will disappear. Sicily, like central Spain, will be too hot and dry for many crops. In Italy and Greece, especially, air pollution will worsen with the rising heat, tourism will falter, and the tide of environmental refugees from Africa will rise and rise.

That's the good news. A new Los Alamos study has announced that, should a meteor happen to fall into the Atlantic (like the one off Yucatan that probably eliminated the dinosaurs sixty-five million years ago), then East Coast urban life would *really* be in trouble. An extreme tsunami would wipe out most settlements within a hundred miles of the coast, from New England to the Carolinas, turning the Poconos and the Berkshires to beachfront. If the meteor should arrive off southern California, then good-bye San Diego, Orange County, and L.A.

Rising Tide

The meteor is unlikely; as unlikely as the chance that any of the futures we now envision will come precisely to pass. But we can know two things about Greater New York five decades hence. First, if the last fifty years are any guide, most of the stresses, dreams, disasters, and component parts of 2050 are already with us—unrecorded, overlooked, misinterpreted, buried on page D24. Second, a rising twenty-first-century ocean and a warmer twenty-first-century climate are no longer academic predictions or developments vaguely on the way. They're here, we invited them, and now we must deal. One former New York City traffic commissioner has already offered some free advice for anyone planning to live in the New York of 2050: better buy stock in a gondola company.

My train home is the Trenton local ("NewYorkNewarkElizabethLindenRahwayMetroParkMetuchenEdisonNewBrunswick JerseyAvenuePrincetonJunctionchangeforPrincetonHamilton . . . aaandTrenton"), and it follows the old Pennsy route, dipping under Hell's Kitchen and the Hudson, then running in darkness until we burst into a Meadowlands doubly gilded. A crimson sun is sinking toward New Jersey's Watchung range, first cousin to Central Park's lost Alps, even as a full silver moon—the hunter's moon, New York colonists would have called it—soars above the asbestos outcrops of Staten Island. The Hudson rail tunnel is almost a century old now, one track in, one track out, and to let an express go by, my commuter train stops, as always, on the embankment beside the National Retail trucking lot, not ten yards from the sleeping rubble of another New York. Under the eighteen-wheelers, earth and water and toxins and time are persuading Bronx tenement bricks into mud and dust once more, grinding glass from a prewar Queens apartment again into sand, blurring chiseled Manhattan stone to elemental granite. You cannot step in the same city twice. But I can still see Marijke's chalk outlines, densely annotated with numbers and arrows, runes on the asphalt for the diggers to come. Beside the train tracks, a stand of native saltgrass bends above water dark as peat and bright as pewter.

I watch the last light touch and leave and touch again the city skyline and I know (although I cannot see) the wild night beginning there: the commuter rats trotting blithely to work, the Wall Street peregrines sailing above the lost Minetta, the midtown skyscrapers swaying in the May wind like giant trees, the horseshoe crabs of the continental shelf turning once more toward the Brooklyn shore, the Bronx coyotes watching the great bridges and waiting for dark. The train begins to move again, across the Secaucus waterlands. The truck lot crowded with eagles, caryatids, sunflowers, falls away. As we turn west toward Newark I cling to the swaying leather seat and look toward Manhattan once more, but the twilight is tricky today. I see only a tangled bank; a green cliff above the estuary; a glitter of minerals on a rising sea. Below the railroad tracks, among the reeds, a bittern waits.

Acknowledgments

For advice and encouragement in exploring the other New York, my thanks to the students and faculty of New York University's Department of Journalism, especially Michael Norman, Mary Quigley, and William Serrin, and to Robert Wilson and the staff of *Preservation* magazine at the National Trust for Historic Preservation in Washington, D.C. The New York Department of Environmental Protection, the New York City Parks Department, the New York City branch of the Audubon Society, and the New Jersey Conservation Foundation were particularly helpful as well. All statistics and findings cited come from the professional literatures of urban ecology, urban history, urban and regional development, geography, wildlife biology, environmental restoration, architecture, political science, cultural studies, environmental science and environmental history, or from multisourced reports by major news organizations. Urban and environmental research sponsored by the United Nations, the U.S. Congress, many federal and state agencies, and the New York Academy of Sciences all proved invalu-

Acknowledgments

able, as did the work (and advice) of environmental and urban experts at the following institutions: Columbia University, Princeton University, New York University, Rutgers University, Montclair State University, and the City University of New York.

But this book is really for Becky Saletan and Cynthia Cannell, who waited, and for Will, who always knew.